501
Geometry Questions

501

Geometry Questions

NEW YORK

Library of Congress Cataloging-in-Publication Data:
McLean, Kerry.
   501 geometry questions / Kerry McLean.—1st ed.
      p. cm.
Summary: Provides practice exercises to help students prepare for multiple-choice tests,
high school exit exams, and other standardized tests on the subject of geometry. Includes
explanations of the answers and simple definitions to reinforce math facts.
   ISBN 1-57685-425-6 (pbk. : alk. paper)
   1. Geometry—Problems, exercises, etc. [1. Geometry—Problems, exercises, etc.]
   I. Title: Five hundred and one geometry questions. II. Title: Five hundred and one
   geometry questions. III. Title.
QA459 .M37 2002
516'.0076—dc21   2002006239

Printed in the United States of America
9 8 7 6 5 4 3 2 1
First Edition

ISBN 1-57685-425-6

For more information or to place an order, contact Learning Express at:
   900 Broadway
   Suite 604
   New York, NY 10003

Or visit us at:
   www.learnatest.com

The LearningExpress Skill Builder in Focus Writing Team is comprised of experts in test preparation, as well as educators and teachers who specialize in language arts and math.

LearningExpress Skill Builder in Focus Writing Team

Brigit Dermott
Freelance Writer
English Tutor, New York Cares
New York, New York

Sandy Gade
Project Editor
LearningExpress
New York, New York

Kerry McLean
Project Editor
Math Tutor
Shirley, New York

William Recco
Middle School Math Teacher, Grade 8
New York Shoreham/Wading River School District
Math Tutor
St. James, New York

Colleen Schultz
Middle School Math Teacher, Grade 8
Vestal Central School District
Math Tutor
Vestal, New York

Contents

Introduction

Geometry is the study of figures in space. As you study geometry, you will measure these figures and determine how they relate to each other and the space they are in. To work with geometry you must understand the difference between representations on the page and the figures they symbolize. What you see is not always what is there. In space, lines define a square; on the page, four distinct black marks define a square. What is the difference? On the page, lines are visible. In space, lines are invisible because lines do not occupy space, in and of themselves. Let this be your first lesson in geometry: Appearances may deceive.

Sadly, for those of you who love the challenge of proving the validity of geometric postulates and theorems—these are the statements that define the rules of geometry—this book is not for you. It will not address geometric proofs or zigzag through tricky logic problems, but it will focus on the practical application of geometry towards solving planar (two-dimensional) spatial puzzles. As you use this book, you will work under the assumption that every definition, every postulate, and every theorem is "infallibly" true.

How to Use This Book

Review the introduction to each chapter before answering the questions in that chapter. Problems toward the end of this book will demand that you apply multiple lessons to solve a question, so be sure to know the preceding chapters well. Take your time; refer to the introductions of each chapter as frequently as you need to, and be sure to understand the answer explanations at the end of each section. This book provides the practice; you provide the initiative and perseverance.

Author's Note

Some geometry books read like instructions on how to launch satellites into space. While geometry is essential to launching NASA space probes, a geometry book should read like instructions on how to make a peanut butter and jelly sandwich. It's not that hard, and after you are done, you should be able to enjoy the product of your labor. Work through this book, enjoy some pb and j, and soon you too can launch space missions if you want.

501
Geometry Questions

1

The Basic Building Blocks of Geometry

Before you can tackle geometry's toughest "stuff," you must understand geometry's simplest "stuff": the point, the line, and the plane. Points, lines, and planes do not occupy space. They are intangible, invisible, and indefinable; yet they determine all tangible visible objects. Trust that they exist, or the next twenty lessons are moot.

Let's get to the point!

Point

Point A

• A   •A

Figure   Symbol

A **point** is a location in space; it indicates position. It occupies no space of its own, and it has no dimension of its own.

Line

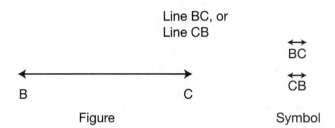

Line BC, or
Line CB

$\overleftrightarrow{BC}$

$\overleftrightarrow{CB}$

B   C

Figure   Symbol

A **line** is a set of continuous points infinitely extending in opposite directions. It has infinite length, but no depth or width.

Plane

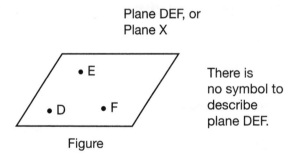

Plane DEF, or
Plane X

• E

• D   • F

There is
no symbol to
describe
plane DEF.

Figure

A **plane** is a flat expanse of points expanding in every direction. Planes have two dimensions: length and width. They do not have depth.

As you probably noticed, each "definition" above builds upon the "definition" before it. There is the point; then there is a series of points; then there is an expanse of points. In geometry, space is pixilated much like the image you see on a TV screen. Be aware that definitions from this point on will build upon each other much like these first three definitions.

Collinear/Noncollinear

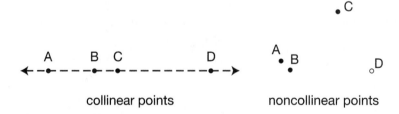

collinear points   noncollinear points

Collinear points are points that form a single straight line when they are connected (two points are always collinear). **Noncollinear points** are points that do not form a single straight line when they are connected (only three or more points can be noncollinear).

Coplanar/Noncoplanar

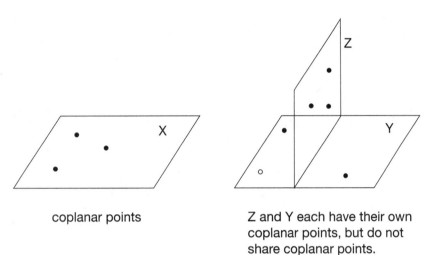

coplanar points

Z and Y each have their own coplanar points, but do not share coplanar points.

Coplanar points are points that occupy the same plane. **Noncoplanar points** are points that do not occupy the same plane.

Ray

Ray GH

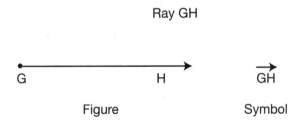

G   H $\overrightarrow{GH}$

Figure   Symbol

A **ray** begins at a point (called an *endpoint* because it marks the *end* of a ray), and infinitely extends in one direction.

Opposite Rays

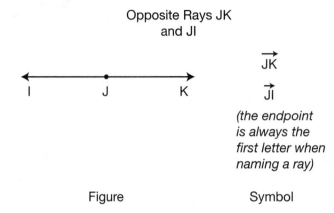

Opposite Rays JK
and JI

$\overrightarrow{JK}$

$\overrightarrow{JI}$

*(the endpoint
is always the
first letter when
naming a ray)*

Figure   Symbol

Opposite rays are rays that share an endpoint and infinitely extend in opposite directions. Opposite rays form straight angles.

Angles

Angle M, or LMN,
or NML, or 1

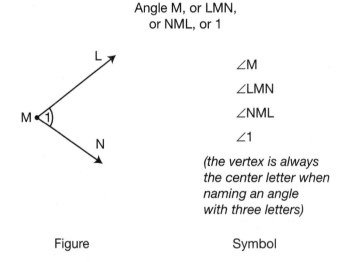

$\angle M$

$\angle LMN$

$\angle NML$

$\angle 1$

*(the vertex is always
the center letter when
naming an angle
with three letters)*

Figure   Symbol

Angles are rays that share an endpoint but infinitely extend in different directions.

Line Segment

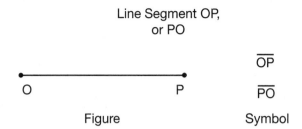

A **line segment** is part of a line with two endpoints. Although not infinitely extending in either direction, the line segment has an infinite set of points between its endpoints.

Set 1

Choose the best answer.

1. Plane geometry
   a. has only two dimensions.
   b. manipulates cubes and spheres.
   c. cannot be represented on the page.
   d. is ordinary.

2. A single location in space is called a
   a. line.
   b. point.
   c. plane.
   d. ray.

3. A single point
   a. has width.
   b. can be accurately drawn.
   c. can exist at multiple planes.
   d. makes a line.

4. A line, plane, ray, and line segment all have
   a. length and depth.
   b. points.
   c. endpoints.
   d. no dimension.

5. Two points determine
   a. a line.
   b. a plane.
   c. a square.
   d. No determination can be made.

6. Three noncollinear points determine
   a. a ray.
   b. a plane.
   c. a line segment.
   d. No determination can be made.

7. Any four points determine
   a. a plane.
   b. a line.
   c. a ray.
   d. No determination can be made.

Set 2

Choose the best answer.

8. Collinear points
   a. determine a plane.
   b. are circular.
   c. are noncoplanar.
   d. are coplanar.

9. How many distinct lines can be drawn through two points?
   a. 0
   b. 1
   c. 2
   d. an infinite number of lines

10. Lines are always
    a. solid.
    b. finite.
    c. noncollinear.
    d. straight.

11. The shortest distance between any two points is
    a. a line.
    b. a line segment.
    c. a ray.
    d. an arch.

12. Which choice below has the most points?
    a. a line
    b. a line segment
    c. a ray
    d. No determination can be made.

Set 3

Answer questions 13 through 16 using the figure below.

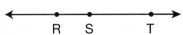

13. There are three different ways to name the line above. What are they? Are there still other ways to name the line? If there are, what are they? If there aren't, why not?

14. Name four different rays. Are there other ways to name each ray? If there are, what are they? If there aren't, why not?

15. Name a pair of opposite rays. Are there other pairs of opposite rays? If there are, what are they?

16. Name three different line segments. Are there other ways to name each line segment? If there are, what are they? If there aren't, why not?

Set 4

Answer questions 17 through 20 using the figure below.

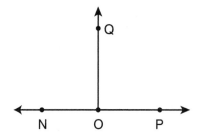

17. There are three different ways to name the line above. What are they? Are there still other ways to name the line? If there are, what are they? If there aren't, why not?

18. Name five different rays. Are there other ways to name each ray? If there are, what are they? If there aren't, why not?

19. Name a pair of opposite rays. Are there other pairs of opposite rays? If there are, what are they?

20. Name three angles. Are there other ways to name each angle? If there are, what are they? If there aren't, why not?

Set 5

Answer questions 21 through 23 using the figure below.

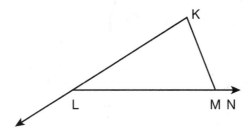

21. Name three different rays. Are there other rays? If there are, what are they?

22. Name five angles. Are there other ways to name each angle? If there are, what are they? If there aren't, why not?

23. Name five different line segments. Are there other ways to name each line segment? If there are, what are they? If there aren't, why not?

Set 6

Ann, Bill, Carl, and Dan work in the same office building. Dan works in the basement while Ann, Bill, and Carl share an office on level X. At any given moment of the day, they are all typing at their desks. Bill likes a window seat; Ann likes to be near the bathroom; and Carl prefers a seat next to the door. Their three cubicles do not line up.

Answer the following questions using the description above.

24. Level X can also be called
    a. Plane Ann, Bill, and Carl.
    b. Plane Ann and Bill.
    c. Plane Dan.
    d. Plane Carl, X, and Bill.

25. If level X represents a plane, then level X has
   a. no points.
   b. only three points.
   c. a finite set of points.
   d. an infinite set of points extending infinitely.

26. If Ann and Bill represent points, then Point Ann
   a. has depth and length, but no width; and is noncollinear with point Bill.
   b. has depth, but no length and width; and is noncollinear with point Bill.
   c. has depth, but no length and width; and is collinear with point Bill.
   d. has no depth, length, and width; and is collinear with point Bill.

27. If Ann, Bill, and Carl represent points, then Points Ann, Bill, and Carl are
   a. collinear and noncoplanar.
   b. noncollinear and coplanar.
   c. noncollinear and noncoplanar.
   d. collinear and coplanar.

28. A line segment drawn between Carl and Dan is
   a. collinear and noncoplanar.
   b. noncollinear and coplanar.
   c. noncollinear and noncoplanar.
   d. collinear and coplanar.

Answers

Set 1

1. **a.** Plane geometry, like its namesake *the plane*, cannot exceed two dimensions. Choice **b** is incorrect because cubes and spheres are three-dimensional. Geometry can be represented on the page—it cannot be accurately drawn, so choice **c** is incorrect. Choice **d** confuses the words *plane* and *plain*.

2. **b.** The definition of a point is "a location in space." Choices **a, c,** and **d** are incorrect because they are all multiple locations in space; the question asks for a "single location in space."

3. **c.** A point by itself can be in any plane. In fact, planes remain undetermined until three noncollinear points exist at once. If you could not guess this, then process of elimination could have brought you to choice **c.** Choices **a** and **b** are incorrect because points are dimensionless; they have no length, width, or depth; they cannot be seen or touched, much less accurately drawn. Just as three points make a plane, two points make a line; consequently choice **d** is incorrect.

4. **b.** Theoretically, space is nothing but infinity of locations, or points. Lines, planes, rays, and line segments are all alignments of points. Lines, rays, and line segments only possess length, so choices **a** and **d** are incorrect. Lines and planes do not have endpoints; choice **c** cannot be the answer either.

5. **a.** Two points determine a line, and only one line can pass any two points. This is commonsensical. Choice **b** is incorrect because it takes three noncollinear points to determine a plane, not two. It also takes a lot more than two points to determine a square, so choice **c** is incorrect.

6. **b.** Three noncollinear points determine a plane. Rays and line segments need collinear points.

7.   **d.** Any four points could determine a number of things: a pair of
     parallel lines, a pair of skewed lines, a plane, and one other
     coplanar/noncoplanar point. Without more information the
     answer cannot be determined.

Set 2

8.   **d.** Collinear points are also coplanar. Choice **a** is not the answer
     because noncollinear points determine planes, not a single line of
     collinear points.

9.   **b.** An infinite number of lines can be drawn through one point,
     but only one straight line can be drawn through two points.

10. **d.** Always assume that in plane geometry a line is a straight line
     unless otherwise stated. Process of elimination works well with this
     question: Lines have one dimension, length, and no substance;
     they are definitely not solid. Lines extend to infinity; they are not
     finite. Finally, we defined noncollinear as a set of points that "do
     not line up"; we take our cue from the last part of that statement.
     Choice **c** is not our answer.

11. **b.** A *line* usually completes this saying, but a line continues
     infinitely. How can something whose length is infinite be short? A
     line segment stops at a point. It alone can be considered the
     shortest distance.

12. **d.** A line, a line segment, and a ray are sets of points. How many
     points make a set? An infinite number. Since a limit cannot be put
     on infinity, not one of the answer choices has more than the other.

Set 3

13. Any six of these names correctly describe the line: $\overleftrightarrow{RS}$, $\overleftrightarrow{SR}$, $\overleftrightarrow{RT}$,
     $\overleftrightarrow{TR}$, $\overleftrightarrow{ST}$, and $\overleftrightarrow{TS}$. Any two points on a given line, regardless of
     their order, describes that line.

14. Two of the four rays can each be called by only one name: $\overrightarrow{ST}$ and
     $\overrightarrow{SR}$. Ray names $\overrightarrow{RT}$ and $\overrightarrow{RS}$ are interchangeable, as are ray names

$\overrightarrow{TS}$ and $\overrightarrow{TR}$; each pair describes one ray. $\overrightarrow{RT}$ and $\overrightarrow{RS}$ describe a
ray beginning at endpoint R and extending infinitely through •T
and •S. $\overrightarrow{TS}$ and $\overrightarrow{TR}$ describe a ray beginning at endpoint T and
extending infinitely through •S and •R.

15. $\overrightarrow{SR}$ and $\overrightarrow{ST}$ are opposite rays. Of the four rays listed, they are the
only pair of opposite rays; they share an endpoint and extend
infinitely in opposite directions.

16. Line segments have two endpoints and can go by two names. It
does not matter which endpoint comes first. $\overline{RT}$ is $\overline{TR}$; $\overline{RS}$ is $\overline{SR}$;
and $\overline{ST}$ is $\overline{TS}$.

Set 4

17. Any six of these names correctly describes the line: $\overleftrightarrow{NP}, \overleftrightarrow{PN}, \overleftrightarrow{NO},$
$\overleftrightarrow{ON}, \overleftrightarrow{PO}, \overleftrightarrow{OP}$. Any two points on a given line, regardless of their
order, describe that line.

18. Three of the five rays can each be called by only one name: $\overrightarrow{OP}$,
$\overrightarrow{ON}$, and $\overrightarrow{OQ}$. Ray-names $\overrightarrow{NO}$ and $\overrightarrow{NP}$ are interchangeable, as
are ray names $\overrightarrow{PO}$ and $\overrightarrow{PN}$; each pair describes one ray each. $\overrightarrow{NO}$
and $\overrightarrow{NP}$ describe a ray beginning at endpoint N and extending
infinitely through •O and •P. $\overrightarrow{PO}$ and $\overrightarrow{PN}$ describe a ray beginning
at end point P and extending infinitely through •O and •N.

19. $\overrightarrow{ON}$ and $\overrightarrow{OP}$ are opposite rays. Of the five rays listed, they are the
only pair of opposite rays; they share an endpoint and extend
infinitely in opposite directions.

20. Angles have two sides, and unless a number is given to describe the
angle, angles can have two names. In our case ∠NOQ is ∠QON;
∠POQ is ∠QOP; and ∠NOP is ∠PON (in case you missed this
one, ∠NOP is a straight angle). Letter O cannot by itself name any
of these angles because all three angles share •O as their vertex.

Set 5

21. Two of the three rays can each be called by only one name: $\overrightarrow{KL}$ and $\overrightarrow{MN}$. $\overrightarrow{LN}$ and $\overrightarrow{LM}$ are interchangeable because they both describe a ray beginning at endpoint L and extending infinitely through •M and •N.

22. Two of the five angles can go by three different names. ∠KLM is ∠MLK is ∠L. ∠LKM is ∠MKL is ∠K. The other three angles can only go by two names each. ∠KMN is ∠NMK. ∠KML is ∠LMK. ∠LMN is ∠NML. Letter M cannot by itself name any of these angles because all three angles share •M as their vertex.

23. Line segments have two endpoints and can go by two names. It makes no difference which endpoint comes first. $\overline{LM}$ is $\overline{ML}$; $\overline{MN}$ is $\overline{NM}$; $\overline{LN}$ is $\overline{NL}$; $\overline{KM}$ is $\overline{MK}$; $\overline{KL}$ is $\overline{LK}$.

Set 6

24. **a.** Three noncollinear points determine a plane. In this case, we know level X is a plane and Ann, Bill, and Carl represent points on that plane. Ann and Bill together are not enough points to define the plane; Dan isn't on plane X and choice **d** doesn't make sense. Choice **a** is the only option.

25. **d.** Unlike a plane, an office floor can hold only so many people; however, imagine the office floor extending infinitely in every direction. How many people could it hold? An infinite number. Like the polygon on the page, level X represents a plane; it is not actually a plane. As a symbol, it acquires the characteristics of that which it symbolizes. Consequently, level X behaves like a plane. For all intents and purposes, it can hold an infinite number of people or points.

26. **d.** Just as the office floor can represent a plane, Ann and Bill can represent points. They acquire the characteristics of a point; and as we know, points have no dimension, and two points make a line.

27. **b.** Ann, Bill, and Carl are all on the same floor, which means they are all on the same plane, and they are not lined up. That makes them noncollinear but coplanar.

28. **d.** Carl and Dan represent two points; two points make a line; and all lines are collinear and coplanar. Granted, Dan and Carl are on two different floors; but remember points exist simultaneously on multiple planes.

2

Types of Angles

Did you ever hear the nursery rhyme about the crooked man who walked a crooked mile? The crooked man was very *angular*. But was he *obtuse* or *acute*?

What's my angle? Just this: angles describe appearances and personalities as well as geometric figures. Review this chapter and consider what angle might best describe you.

Angles

Chapter 1 defines an **angle** as two rays sharing an endpoint and extending infinitely in different directions.

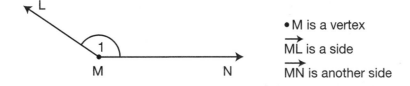

- M is a vertex
- $\overrightarrow{ML}$ is a side
- $\overrightarrow{MN}$ is another side

Special Angles

Angles are measured in degrees; and degrees measure rotation, not distance. Some rotations merit special names. Watch as $\overrightarrow{BA}$ rotates around •B:

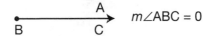 $m\angle ABC = 0$

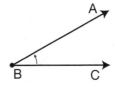 $0 > m\angle ABC < 90,$ ACUTE

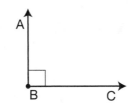 $m\angle ABC = 90,$ RIGHT

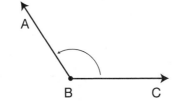 $90 < m\angle ABC < 180,$ OBTUSE

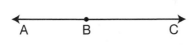 $m\angle ABC = 180,$ STRAIGHT

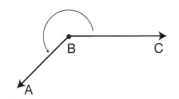 $180 < m\angle ABC < 360,$ REFLEX

Set 7

Choose the answer that *incorrectly* names an angle in each preceding figure.

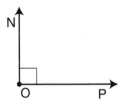

29. a. ∠NOP
   b. ∠PON
   c. ∠O
   d. ∠90°

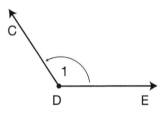

30. a. ∠CDE
   b. ∠CED
   c. ∠D
   d. ∠1

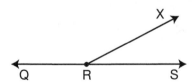

31. a. ∠R
   b. ∠QRS
   c. ∠XRS
   d. ∠XRQ

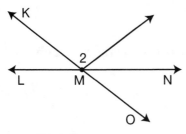

32.   **a.** ∠KMN
      b. ∠NMO
      c. ∠KML
      d. ∠M

Set 8

Choose the best answer.

33. All opposite rays
    a. are also straight angles.
    b. have different end points.
    c. extend in the same direction.
    d. do not form straight lines.

34. Angles that share a common vertex point **cannot**
    a. share a common angle side.
    b. be right angles.
    c. use the vertex letter name as an angle name.
    d. share interior points.

35. ∠EDF and ∠GDE
    a. are the same angle.
    b. only share a common vertex.
    c. are adjacent angles; they share a vertex, a side, and no interior
       points.
    d. share a common side and vertex.

36. ∠ABD is a right angle or
   a. m ∠ABD = 90°.
   b. m∠ABD = 90.
   c. ∠ABD = 90°.
   d. 90° = ABD.

Set 9

Label each angle measurement as acute, right, obtuse, straight, or reflexive.

37. 13.5°

38. 91°

39. 46°

40. 179.3°

41. 355°

42. 180.2°

43. 90°

Set 10

For each diagram in this set, name every angle in as many ways as you can. Then label each angle as acute, right, obtuse, straight, or reflexive.

44.

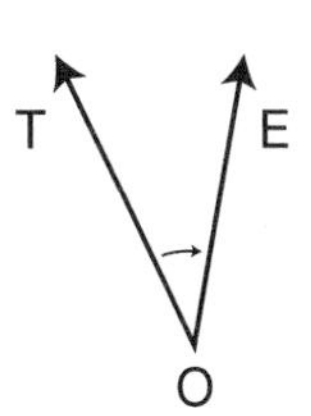

45.

46.

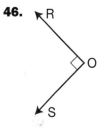

47.

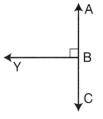

48.

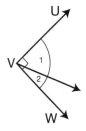

49.

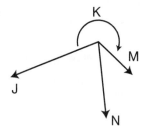

50.

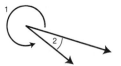

Answers

Set 7

29. **d.** Angles are not named by their measurements.

30. **b.** ∠CED describes an angle whose vertex is •E, not •D.

31. **a.** If a vertex is shared by more than one angle, then the letter describing the vertex cannot be used to name any of the angles. It would be too confusing.

32. **d.** If a vertex is shared by more than one angle, then the letter describing the vertex cannot be used to name any of the angles. It would be too confusing.

Set 8

33. **a.** Opposite rays form straight lines and straight angles. Choices **b**, **c**, and **d** contradict the three defining elements of a pair of opposite rays.

34. **c.** If a vertex is shared by more than one angle, then it cannot be used to name any of the angles.

35. **d.** ∠EDF and ∠GDE share vertex point D and side DE. Choice **c** is incorrect because there is not enough information to determine adjacency.

36. **b.** This is a technicality. Lowercase m means *the measurement of.* Whenever discussing the measurement of an angle, it is good practice to always note it as $m∠$ABD =. Because $m∠$ means *the measurement of ∠ABD is,* you do not need to include a degree (°) sign after the measure is given. An angle can only be measured in degrees. Without lowercase m, you are not stating the angle's measure; you are describing the angle itself.

Set 9

37. $0° < 13.5° < 90°$; acute

38. $90° < 91° < 180°$; obtuse

39. $0° < 46° < 90°$; acute

40. $90° < 179.3° < 180°$; obtuse

41. $180° < 355° < 360°$; reflexive

42. $180° < 180.2° < 360°$; reflexive

43. $90° = 90°$; right

Set 10

44. ∠TOE, ∠EOT, or ∠O; acute

45. ∠1; obtuse

46. ∠ROS, ∠SOR, or ∠O; obtuse

47. ∠ABY or ∠YBA; right
∠YBC or ∠CBY; right
∠ABC and ∠CBA; straight

48. ∠1; acute
∠2; acute
∠UVW or ∠WVU; right

49. ∠NKM or ∠MKN; acute
∠JKM or ∠MKJ; obtuse
∠JKM or ∠MKJ; reflexive
∠JKN or ∠NKJ; acute

50. ∠1; reflexive
∠2; acute

3

Working with Lines

Some lines never cross. **Parallel lines** are coplanar lines that never intersect; they travel similar paths at a constant distance from one another. **Skew lines** are noncoplanar lines that never intersect; they travel dissimilar paths on separate planes.

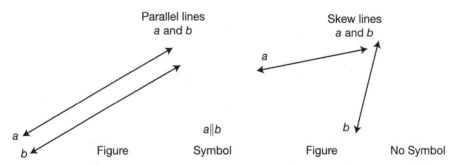

When lines cross, they do not "collide" into each other, nor do they lie one on top of the other. **Lines do not occupy space.** Watch how these lines "cross" each other; they could be considered models of peaceful coexistence (next page).

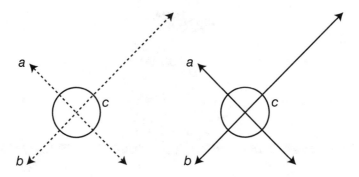

Two-Lined Intersections

When two lines look like they are crossing, they are really sharing a single point. That point is on both lines. When lines intersect, they create four angles: notice the appearance of the hub around the vertex in the figure above. When the measures of those four angles are added, the sum equals the rotation of a complete circle, or 360°.

When the sum of the measures of any two angles equals 180°, the angles are called **supplementary angles**.

Two angles next to each other are called **adjacent angles**. They share a vertex, a side, and no interior points. Adjacent angles along a straight line measure half a circle's rotation, or 180°.

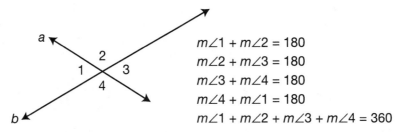

$m\angle1 + m\angle2 = 180$
$m\angle2 + m\angle3 = 180$
$m\angle3 + m\angle4 = 180$
$m\angle4 + m\angle1 = 180$
$m\angle1 + m\angle2 + m\angle3 + m\angle4 = 360$

When straight lines intersect, opposite angles, or angles nonadjacent to each other, are called **vertical angles**. They are always congruent.

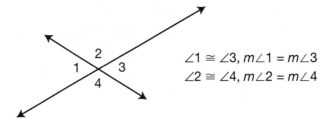

$\angle1 \cong \angle3, m\angle1 = m\angle3$
$\angle2 \cong \angle4, m\angle2 = m\angle4$

When two lines intersect and form four right angles, the lines are considered **perpendicular**.

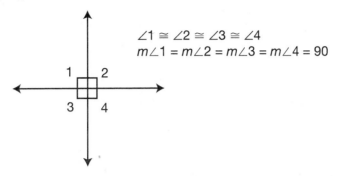

$$\angle 1 \cong \angle 2 \cong \angle 3 \cong \angle 4$$
$$m\angle 1 = m\angle 2 = m\angle 3 = m\angle 4 = 90$$

Three-Lined Intersections

A **transversal line** intersects two or more lines, each at a different point. Because a transversal line crosses at least two other lines, eight or more angles are created. When a transversal intersects a pair of parallel lines, certain angles are always congruent or supplementary. Pairs of these angles have special names:

Corresponding angles are angles in corresponding positions.

Look for a distinctive F shaped figure.

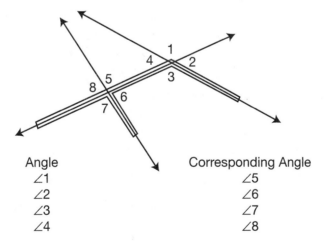

Angle	Corresponding Angle
∠1	∠5
∠2	∠6
∠3	∠7
∠4	∠8

When a transversal intersects a pair of parallel lines, **corresponding angles** are **congruent**.

Interior angles are angles inside a pair of crossed lines.

Look for a distinctive I shaped figure.

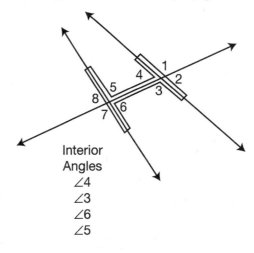

Interior
Angles
∠4
∠3
∠6
∠5

Same-side interior angles are interior angles on the same side of a transversal line.

Look for a distinctive C shaped figure.

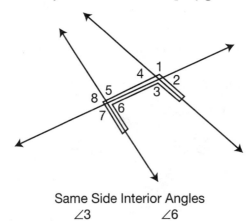

Same Side Interior Angles

∠3	∠6
∠4	∠5

When a transversal intersects a pair of parallel lines, **same-side interior angles** are **supplementary**.

Alternate interior angles are interior angles on opposite sides of a transversal line.

Look for a distinctive Z shaped figure.

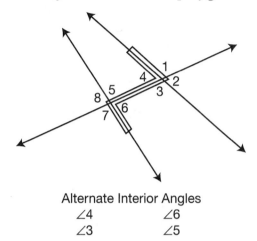

Alternate Interior Angles
∠4   ∠6
∠3   ∠5

When a transversal intersects a pair of parallel lines, **alternate interior angles** are **congruent**.

When a transversal is perpendicular to a pair of parallel lines, all eight angles are congruent.

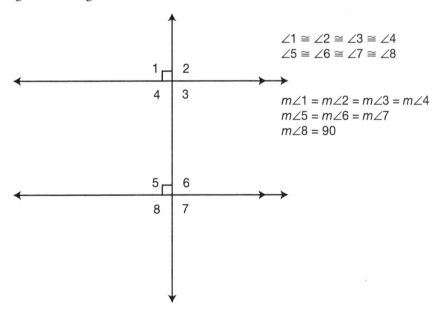

∠1 ≅ ∠2 ≅ ∠3 ≅ ∠4
∠5 ≅ ∠6 ≅ ∠7 ≅ ∠8

$m\angle 1 = m\angle 2 = m\angle 3 = m\angle 4$
$m\angle 5 = m\angle 6 = m\angle 7$
$m\angle 8 = 90$

There are also exterior angles, same-side exterior angles, and alternate exterior angles. They are positioned by the same common-sense rules as the interior angles.

Set 11

Use the following diagram to answer questions 51 through 56.

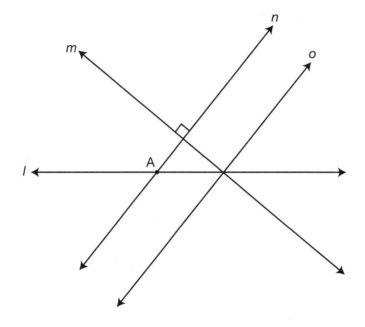

51. Which set of lines are transversals?
 a. *l, m, o*
 b. *o, m, n*
 c. *l, o, n*
 d. *l, m, n*

52. •A is
 a. between lines *l* and *n*.
 b. on lines *l* and *n*.
 c. on line *l*, but not line *n*.
 d. on line *n*, but not line *l*.

53. How many points do line *m* and line *l* share?
 a. 0
 b. 1
 c. 2
 d. infinite

54. Which lines are perpendicular?
   a. *n, m*
   b. *o, l*
   c. *l, n*
   d. *m, l*

55. How many lines can be drawn through •A that are perpendicular to line *l*?
   a. 0
   b. 1
   c. 10,000
   d. infinite

56. How many lines can be drawn through •A that are parallel to line *m*?
   a. 0
   b. 1
   c. 2
   d. infinite

Set 12

Use the following diagram to answer questions 57 through 61.

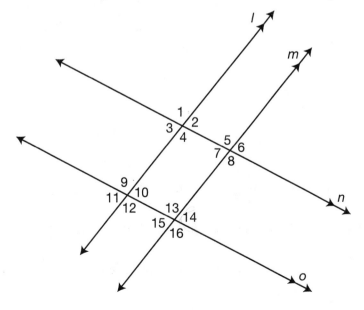

57. In sets, name all the congruent angles.

58. In pairs, name all the vertical angles.

59. In pairs, name all the alternate interior angles.

60. In pairs, name all the corresponding angles.

61. In pairs, name all the angles that are same-side interior.

Set 13

Use the following diagram and the information below to determine if lines *o* and *p* are parallel. Place a checkmark (✓) beside statements that prove lines *o* and *p* are parallel; place an X beside statements that neither prove nor disprove that lines *o* and *p* are parallel.

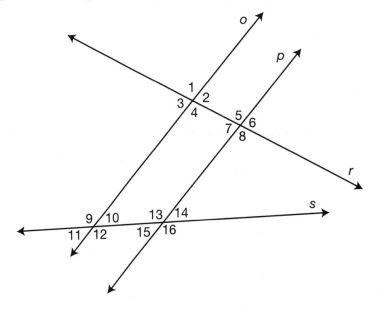

62. If ∠5 and ∠4 are congruent and equal, then _____.

63. If ∠1 and ∠2 are congruent and equal, then _____.

64. If ∠9 and ∠16 are congruent and equal, then _____.

65. If ∠12 and ∠15 are congruent and equal, then _____.

66. If ∠8 and ∠4 are congruent and equal, then _____.

Set 14

Circle the correct answer True or False.

67. Angles formed by a transversal and two parallel lines are either complementary or congruent.   **True or False**

68. When four rays extend from a single endpoint, adjacent angles are always supplementary.   **True or False**

69. Angles supplementary to the same angle or angles with the same measure are also equal in measure.   **True or False**

70. Adjacent angles that are also congruent are always right angles. **True or False**

71. Parallel and skew lines are coplanar.   **True or False**

72. Supplementary angles that are also congruent are right angles. **True or False**

73. If vertical angles are acute, the angle adjacent to them must be obtuse.   **True or False**

74. Vertical angles can be reflexive.   **True or False**

75. Four vertical angles are never congruent.   **True or False**

76. The sum of interior angles formed by a pair of parallel lines crossed by a transversal is always 360°.   **True or False**

77. The sum of exterior angles formed by a pair of parallel lines and a transversal is always 360°.   **True or False**

Answers

Set 11

51. **d.** In order to be a transversal, a line must cut across two other lines at different points. Line *o* crosses lines *m* and *l* at the same point; it is not a transversal.

52. **b.** When two lines intersect, they share a single point in space. That point is technically on both lines.

53. **b.** Lines are straight; they cannot backtrack or bend (if they could bend, they would be a curve, not a line). Consequently, when two lines intersect, they can share only one point.

54. **a.** When intersecting lines create right angles, they are perpendicular.

55. **b.** An infinite number of lines can pass through any given point in space—only one line can pass through a point and be perpendicular to an existing line. In this case, that point is on the line; however, this rule also applies to points that are not on the line.

56. **b.** Only one line can pass through a point and be parallel to an existing line.

Set 12

57. $\angle 1 \cong \angle 4 \cong \angle 5 \cong \angle 8 \cong \angle 9 \cong \angle 12 \cong \angle 13 \cong \angle 16$;
    $\angle 2 \cong \angle 3 \cong \angle 6 \cong \angle 7 \cong \angle 10 \cong \angle 11 \cong \angle 14 \cong \angle 15$

58. $\angle 1, \angle 4$; $\angle 2, \angle 3$; $\angle 5, \angle 8$; $\angle 6, \angle 7$; $\angle 9, \angle 12$; $\angle 10, \angle 11$; $\angle 13, \angle 16$; $\angle 14, \angle 15$

59. $\angle 1, \angle 9$; $\angle 2, \angle 10$; $\angle 3, \angle 11$; $\angle 4, \angle 12$; $\angle 5, \angle 13$; $\angle 6, \angle 14$; $\angle 7, \angle 15$; $\angle 8, \angle 16$

60. $\angle 3, \angle 10$; $\angle 4, \angle 9$; $\angle 7, \angle 14$; $\angle 8, \angle 13$

61. $\angle 3, \angle 9$; $\angle 4, \angle 10$; $\angle 7, \angle 13$; $\angle 8, \angle 14$

Set 13

62. ✓. Only three congruent angle pairs can prove a pair of lines cut
    by a transversal are parallel: alternate interior angles, alternate
    exterior angles, and corresponding angles. Angles 5 and 4 are
    alternate interior angles—notice the Z figure.

63. X. ∠1 and ∠2 are adjacent angles. Their measurements combined
    must equal 180°, but they do not determine parallel lines.

64. ✓. ∠9 and ∠16 are alternate exterior angles.

65. X. ∠12 and ∠15 are same side interior angles; they do not
    determine parallel lines.

66. ✓. ∠8 and ∠4 are corresponding angles.

Set 14

67. **False.** The angles of a pair of parallel lines cut by a transversal are
    always either supplementary or congruent, meaning their
    measurements either add up to 180°, or they are the same measure.

68. **False.** If the four rays made two pairs of opposite rays, then this
    statement would be true; however, any four rays extending from a
    single point do not have to line up into a pair of straight lines; and
    without a pair of straight lines there are no supplementary angle
    pairs.

69. True.

70. **False.** Adjacent angles do not always form straight lines; to be
    adjacent, angles need to share a vertex, a side, and no interior
    points. However, adjacent angles that do form a straight line are
    always right angles.

71. **False.** Parallel lines are coplanar; skew lines are not.

72. **True.** A pair of supplementary angles must measure 180°. If the pair is also congruent, they must measure 90° each. An angle that measures 90° is a right angle.

73. **True.** When two lines intersect, they create four angles. The two angles opposite each other are congruent. Adjacent angles are supplementary. If vertical angles are acute, angles adjacent to them must be obtuse in order to measure 180°.

74. **False.** Vertical angles cannot be equal to or more than 180°; otherwise, they could not form supplementary angle pairs with their adjacent angle.

75. **False.** Perpendicular lines form all right angles.

76. **True.** Adjacent interior angles form supplementary pairs; their joint measurement is 180°. Two sets of adjacent interior angles must equal 360°.

77. **True.** Two sets of adjacent exterior angles must equal 360°.

4

Measuring Angles

Had enough of angles? You haven't even begun! You named angles and determined their congruence or incongruence when two or more lines crossed. In this chapter, you will actually measure angles using an instrument called the **protractor**.

How to Measure an Angle Using a Protractor

Place the center point of the protractor over the angle's vertex. Keeping these points affixed, position the base of the protractor over one of the two angle sides. Protractors have two scales—choose the scale that starts with 0 on the side you have chosen. Where the second arm of your angle crosses the scale on the protractor is your measurement.

How to Draw an Angle Using a Protractor

To draw an angle, first draw a ray. The ray's end point becomes the angle's vertex. Position the protractor as if you were measuring an angle. Choose your scale and make a mark on the page at the desired measurement.

Remove the protractor and connect the mark you made to the vertex with a straight edge. Voilà, you have an angle.

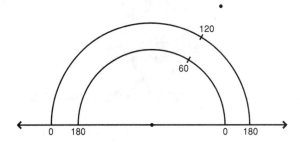

Adjacent Angles

Adjacent angles share a vertex, a side, and no interior points; they are angles that lie side-by-side.

   Note: Because adjacent angles share a single vertex point, adjacent angles can be added together to make larger angles. This technique will be particularly useful when working with **complementary** and **supplementary** angles in Chapter 5.

Set 15

Using the diagram below, measure each angle.

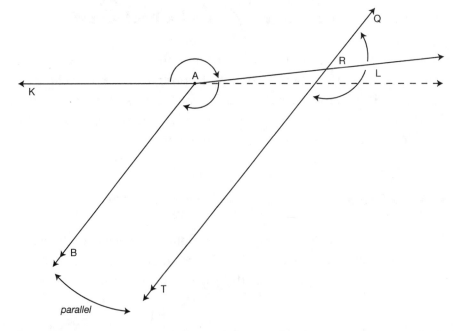

78. ∠LRQ

79. ∠ART

80. ∠KAL

81. ∠KAB

82. ∠LAB

Set 16

Using a protractor, draw a figure starting with question 83. Complete the figure with question 87.

83. Draw $\overrightarrow{EC}$.

84. $\overrightarrow{ED}$ rotates 43° counterclockwise (left) from $\overrightarrow{EC}$. Draw $\overrightarrow{ED}$.

85. $\overrightarrow{EF}$ rotates 90° counterclockwise from $\overrightarrow{ED}$. Draw $\overrightarrow{EF}$.

86. $\overrightarrow{EG}$ and $\overrightarrow{EF}$ are opposite rays. Draw $\overrightarrow{EG}$.

87. Measure ∠DEG.

Set 17

Choose the best answer.

88. ∠ROT and ∠POT are
   a. supplementary angles.
   b. complementary angles.
   c. congruent angles.
   d. adjacent angles.
   e. No determination can be made.

89. When adjacent angles RXZ and ZXA are added, they make
  a. ∠RXA.
  b. ∠XZ.
  c. ∠XRA.
  d. ∠ARX.
  e. No determination can be made.

90. Adjacent angles EBA and EBC make ∠ABC. ∠ABC measures 132°. ∠EBA measures 81°. ∠EBC must measure
  a. 213°.
  b. 61°.
  c. 51°.
  d. 48°.
  e. No determination can be made.

91. ∠SVT and ∠UVT are adjacent supplementary angles. ∠SVT measures 53°. ∠UVT must measure
  a. 180°.
  b. 233°.
  c. 133°.
  d. 127°.
  e. No determination can be made.

92. ∠AOE is a straight angle. ∠BOE is a right angle. ∠AOB is
  a. a reflexive angle.
  b. an acute angle.
  c. an obtuse angle.
  d. a right angle.
  e. No determination can be made.

Set 18

A **bisector** is any ray or line segment that divides an angle or another line segment into two congruent and equal parts.

In Anglesville, Avenues A, B, and C meet at Town Hall (T). Avenues A and C extend in opposite directions from Town Hall; they form one straight avenue extending infinitely. Avenue B is 68° from Avenue C. The Anglesville Town Board wants to construct two more avenues to meet at Town

Hall, Avenues Z and Y. Avenue Y would bisect the angle between Avenues B and C; Avenue Z would bisect the angle between Avenues A and B.

Answer the following questions using the description above.

93. What is the measure between Avenue Y and Avenue Z? What is the special name for this angle?

94. A new courthouse opened on Avenue Y. An alley connects the courthouse to Avenue C perpendicularly. What is the measure of the angle between Avenue Y and the alley (the three angles inside a closed three-sided figure equal 180°)?

Answers

Set 15

78. $m\angle LRQ = 45$

79. $m\angle ART = 45$

80. $m\angle KAL = 174$

81. $m\angle KAB = 51$

82. $m\angle LAB = 135$

Set 16

83.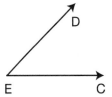

84.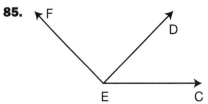

85.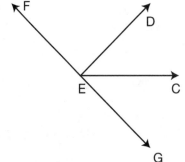

86.

87. $m\angle DEG = 90$

Set 17

88. **e.** $\angle ROT$ and $\angle POT$ share a vertex point and one angle side. However, it cannot be determined that they do not share any interior points, that they form a straight line, that they form a right angle, or that they are the same shape and size. The answer must be choice **e.**

89. **a.** When angles are added together to make larger angles, the vertex always remains the same. Choices **c** and **d** remove the vertex point to •R; consequently, they are incorrect. Choice **b** does not name the vertex at all, so it is also incorrect. Choice **e** is incorrect because we are given that the angles are adjacent; we know they share side XZ; and we know they do not share sides XR and XA. This is enough information to determine the $\angle RXA$.

90. **c.** EQUATION:
$m\angle ABC - m\angle EBA = m\angle EBC$
$132 - 81 = 51$

91. **d.** EQUATION:
$m\angle SVT + m\angle UVT = 180$
$53 + m\angle UVT = 180$
$m\angle UVT = 127$

92. **d.** Draw this particular problem out; any which way you draw it, $\angle AOB$ and $\angle BOE$ are supplementary. 90° subtracted from 180° equals 90°. $\angle AOB$ is a right angle.

Set 18

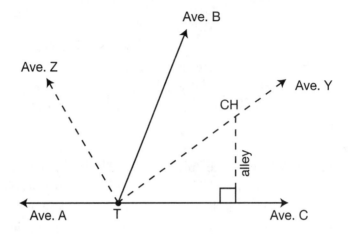

Map of Anglesville

93. Bisect means *cuts in half or divides in half.*

EQUATIONS:

$m\angle BTC = 68$; half of $m\angle BTC = 34$

$m\angle BTA = 180 - m\angle BTC$

$m\angle BTA = 112$; half of $m\angle BTA = 56$

$m\angle ZTB + m\angle BTY = m\angle ZTY$

$56 + 34 = 90$

$\angle YTZ$ is a right angle.

94. Add the alley to your drawing. $m\angle$Avenue Y, Courthouse, alley is $180 - (90 + m\angle YTC)$ or 56.

5

Pairs of Angles

Well done! Good job! Excellent work! You have mastered the use of protractors. You can now move into an entire chapter dedicated to complements and supplements. Perhaps the three most useful angle pairs to know in geometry are complementary, supplementary, and vertical angle pairs.

Complementary Angles

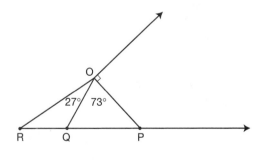

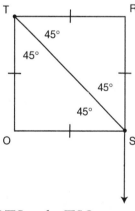

∠ROQ and ∠QOP are adjacent angles
$m\angle$ ROQ + m ∠QOP = 90

∠OTS and ∠TSO are
nonadjacent angles
$m\angle$OTS + $m\angle$TSO = 90

When two adjacent or nonadjacent angles have a total measure of 90°, they are **complementary angles**.

Supplementary Angles

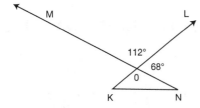   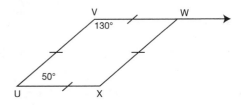

∠MOL and ∠LON are
adjacent straight angles
$m∠MOL + m∠ LON = 180$

∠XUV and ∠UVW are non-
adjacent angles
$m∠XUV + m∠UVW = 180$

When two adjacent or nonadjacent angles have a total measure of 180° they are **supplementary angles**.

Vertical Angles

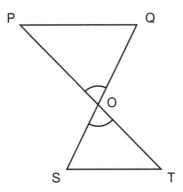

∠POT and ∠QOS are straight angles
∠POQ ≅ ∠SOT $m∠POQ = m∠SOT$
∠POS ≅ ∠QOT $m∠POS = m∠QOT$

When two straight lines intersect or when two pairs of opposite rays extend from the same endpoint, opposite angles (angles nonadjacent to each other), they are called **vertical angles**. They are always congruent.

Other Angles That Measure 180°

When a line crosses a pair of parallel lines, **interior angles** are angles inside the parallel lines. When three line segments form a closed figure, interior angles are the angles inside that closed figure.

Very important: The total of a triangle's three interior angles is always 180°.

Set 19

Choose the best answer for questions 95 through 99 based on the figure below.

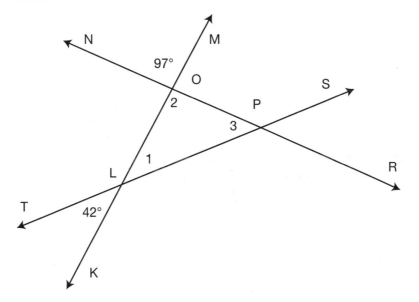

95. Name the angle vertical to ∠NOL.
   a. ∠NOL
   b. ∠KLP
   c. ∠LOP
   d. ∠MOP

96. Name the angle vertical to ∠TLK.
   a. ∠MOR
   b. ∠NOK
   c. ∠KLT
   d. ∠MLS

97. Name the pair of angles supplementary to ∠NOM.
  a. ∠MOR and ∠NOK
  b. ∠SPR and ∠TPR
  c. ∠NOL and ∠LOP
  d. ∠TLK and ∠KLS

98. ∠1, ∠2, and ∠3 respectively measure
  a. 90°, 40°, 140°.
  b. 139°, 41°, 97°.
  c. 42°, 97°, 41°.
  d. 41°, 42°, 83°.

99. The measure of exterior ∠OPS is
  a. 139°.
  b. 83°.
  c. 42°.
  d. 41°.

Set 20

Choose the best answer.

100. If ∠LKN and ∠NOP are complementary angles,
  a. they are both acute.
  b. they must both measure 45°.
  c. they are both obtuse.
  d. one is acute and the other is obtuse.
  e. No determination can be made.

101. If ∠KAT and ∠GIF are supplementary angles,
  a. they are both acute.
  b. they must both measure 90°.
  c. they are both obtuse.
  d. one is acute and the other is obtuse.
  e. No determination can be made.

102. If ∠DEF and ∠IPN are congruent, they are
   a. complementary angles.
   b. supplementary angles.
   c. right angles.
   d. adjacent angles.
   e. No determination can be made.

103. If ∠ABE and ∠GIJ are congruent supplementary angles, they are
   a. acute angles.
   b. obtuse angles.
   c. right angles.
   d. adjacent angles.
   e. No determination can be made.

104. If ∠EDF and ∠HIJ are supplementary angles, and ∠SUV and
   ∠EDF are also supplementary angles, then ∠HIJ and ∠SUV are
   a. acute angles.
   b. obtuse angles.
   c. right angles.
   d. congruent angles.
   e. No determination can be made.

Set 21

**Fill in the blanks based on your knowledge of angles and the figure
below.**

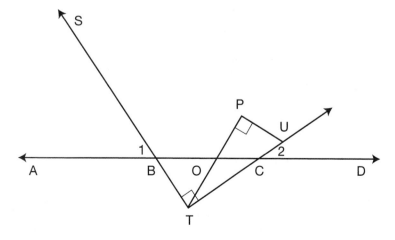

105. If ∠ABT is obtuse, ∠TBO is _____.

106. ∠BTO and ∠OTC are _____.

107. If ∠POC is acute, ∠BOP is _____.

108. If ∠1 is congruent to ∠2, then _____.

Set 22

State the relationship or sum of the angles given based on the figure below. If a relationship cannot be determined, then state, "They cannot be determined."

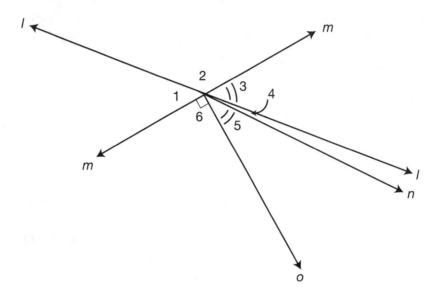

109. Measurement of ∠2 plus the measures of ∠6 and ∠5.

110. ∠1 and ∠3.

111. ∠1 and ∠2.

112. The sum of ∠5, ∠4, and ∠3.

113. ∠6 and ∠2.

114. The sum of ∠1, ∠6, and ∠5.

Answers

Set 19

95. c. ∠NOM and ∠LOP are opposite angles formed by intersecting lines NR and MK; thus, they are vertical angles.

96. d. ∠TLK and ∠MLS are opposite angles formed by intersecting lines TS and MK; thus, they are vertical angles.

97. a. ∠MOR and ∠NOK are both adjacent to ∠NOM along two different lines. The measure of each angle added to the measure of ∠NOM equals that of a straight line, or 180°. Each of the other answer choices is supplementary to each other, but not to ∠NOM.

98. c. ∠1 is the vertical angle to ∠TLK, which is given. ∠2 is the vertical pair to ∠NOM, which is also given. Since vertical angles are congruent, ∠1 and ∠2 measure 42° and 97°, respectively. To find the measure of ∠3, subtract the sum of ∠1 and ∠2 from 180° (the sum of the measure of a triangle's interior angles):
$180 - (42 + 97) = m\angle 3$
$41 = m\angle 3$

99. a. There are two ways to find the measure of exterior angle OPS. The first method subtracts the measure of ∠3 from 180°. The second method adds the measures of ∠1 and ∠2 together because the measure of an exterior angle equals the sum of the two nonadjacent interior angles. ∠OPS measures 139°.

Set 20

100. a. The sum of any two complementary angles must equal 90°. Any angle less than 90° is acute. It only makes sense that the measure of two acute angles could add to 90°. Choice **b** assumes both angles are also congruent; however, that information is not given. If the measure of one obtuse angle equals more than 90°, then two obtuse angles could not possibly measure exactly 90° together. Choices **c** and **d** are incorrect.

101. **e.** Unlike the question above, where every complementary angle must also be acute, supplementary angles can be acute, right, or obtuse. If an angle is obtuse, its supplement is acute. If an angle is right, its supplement is also right. Two obtuse angles can never be a supplementary pair, and two acute angles can never be a supplementary pair. Without more information, this question cannot be determined.

102. **e.** Complementary angles that are also congruent measure 45° each. Supplementary angles that are also congruent measure 90° each. Without more information, this question cannot be determined.

103. **c.** Congruent supplementary angles always measure 90° each:
$m\angle ABE = x$
$m\angle GIJ = x$
$m\angle ABE + m\angle GIJ = 180$; replace each angle with its measure:
$x + x = 180$
$2x = 180$; divide each side by 2:
$x = 90$
Any 90° angle is a right angle.

104. **d.** When two angles are supplementary to the same angle, they are congruent to each other:
$m\angle EDF + m\angle HIJ = 180$
$m\angle EDF + m\angle SUV = 180$
$m\angle EDF + m\angle HIJ = m\angle SUV + m\angle EDF$; subtract $m\angle EDF$
from each side:
$m\angle HIJ = m\angle SUV$

Set 21

105. **Acute.** $\angle ABT$ and $\angle TBO$ are adjacent angles on the same line. As a supplementary pair, the sum of their measures must equal 180°. If one angle is more than 90°, the other angle must compensate by being less than 90°. Thus if one angle is obtuse, the other angle is acute.

106. **Adjacent complementary angles.** $\angle BTO$ and $\angle OTC$ share a side, a vertex, and no interior points; they are adjacent. The sum of their measures must equal 90° because they form a right angle; thus, they are complementary.

107. **Obtuse.** ∠POC and ∠POB are adjacent angles on the same line. As a supplementary pair, the sum of their measures must equal 180°. If one angle is less than 90°, the other angle must compensate by being more than 90°. Thus if one angle is acute, the other angle is obtuse.

108. **∠SBO and ∠OCU are congruent.** When two angles are supplementary to the same angle or angles that measure the same, then they are congruent.

Set 22

109. **Equal.** Together ∠5 and ∠6 form the vertical angle pair to ∠2. Consequently, the angles are congruent and their measurements are equal.

110. **A determination cannot be made.** ∠1 and ∠3 may look like vertical angles, but do not be deceived. Vertical angle pairs are formed when lines intersect. The vertical angle to ∠1 is the full angle that is opposite and between lines *m* and *l*.

111. **Adjacent supplementary angles.** ∠1 and ∠2 share a side, a vertex and no interior points; they are adjacent. The sum of their measures must equal 180° because they form a straight line; thus they are supplementary.

112. **90°.** ∠6, ∠5, ∠4, and ∠3 are on a straight line. All together, they measure 180°. If ∠6 is a right angle, it equals 90°. The remaining three angles must equal 180° minus 90°, or 90°.

113. **A determination cannot be made.** ∠6 and ∠2 may look like vertical angles, but vertical pairs are formed when lines intersect. The vertical angle to ∠2 is the full angle that is opposite and between lines *m* and *l*.

114. **180°.**

6

Types of Triangles

Mathematicians have an old joke about angles being very friendly. How so? Because they are always open! The two rays of an angle extend out in different directions and continue on forever. On the other hand, polygons are the introverts in mathematics. If you connect three or more line segments end-to-end, what do you have? A very shy *closed-figure*.

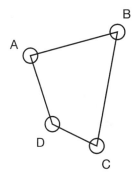

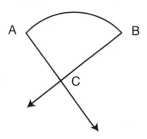

Polygon

- made of all line segments
- each line segment exclusively meets the end of another line segment
- all line segments make a closed figure

NOT a Polygon

- $\overset{\frown}{AB}$ is not a line segment
- C is not an endpoint
- Figure ABC is not a closed figure ($\overrightarrow{AC}$ and $\overrightarrow{BC}$ extend infinitely)

Closed-figures are better known as **polygons**; and the simplest polygon is the triangle. It has the fewest sides and angles that a polygon can have.

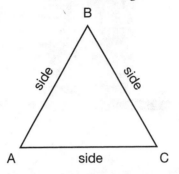

ΔABC

Sides: $\overline{AB}$, $\overline{BC}$ and $\overline{CA}$

Vertices: ∠ABC, ∠BCA, and ∠CAB

Triangles can be one of three special types depending upon the congruence or incongruence of its three sides.

Naming Triangles by Their Sides

Scalene   no congruent sides   no congruent angles

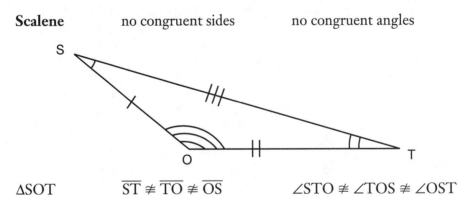

ΔSOT $\overline{ST} \neq \overline{TO} \neq \overline{OS}$ ∠STO ≆ ∠TOS ≆ ∠OST

Isosceles   two congruent sides   two congruent angles

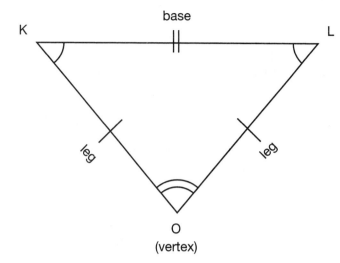

base

K   L

leg   leg

O
(vertex)

ΔKLO $\overline{KO} \cong \overline{LO}$ ∠LKO ≅ ∠KLO

Equilateral   three congruent sides   three congruent angles

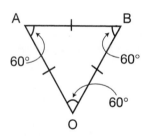

A   B

60°   60°

60°

O

ΔABO $\overline{AB} \cong \overline{BO} \cong \overline{OA}$ ∠ABO ≅ ∠BOA ≅ ∠BAO

Naming Triangles by Their Angles

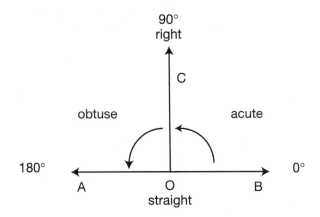

Acute Triangles   three acute angles

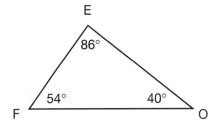

Scalene Triangle EOF $m\angle$EOF, $m\angle$OFE
                             and $m\angle$FEO < 90

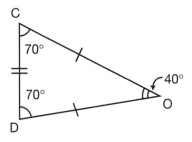

Isosceles Triangle COD $m\angle$COD, $m\angle$ODC
                             and $m\angle$DCO < 90

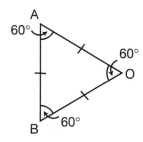

Equilateral Triangle ABO $m\angle$ABO, $m\angle$BOA
Note: Each angle is equal to 60°.   and $m\angle$OAB < 90

Equiangular Triangle   three congruent angles

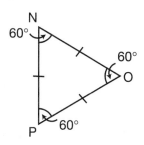

Equilateral Triangle NOP $\angle$NOP $\cong$ $\angle$OPN $\cong$ $\angle$PNO

Right Triangle   one right angle   two acute angles

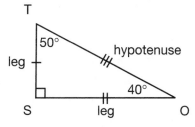

Scalene Triangle TOS $m\angle$TSO = 90 $m\angle$TOS and $m\angle$STO < 90

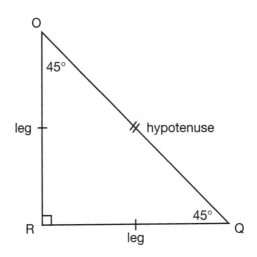

Isosceles Triangle ORQ $m\angle ORQ = 90$ $m\angle ROQ$ and $m\angle RQO < 90$

Obtuse Triangle   one obtuse angle   two acute angles

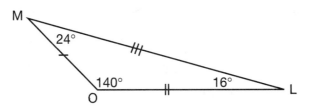

Scalene Triangle LMO $m\angle LOM > 90$ $m\angle OLM$ and $m\angle LMO < 90$

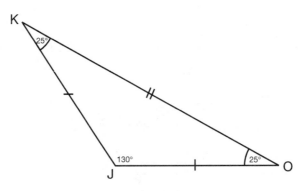

Isosceles Triangle JKO $m\angle OJK > 90$ $m\angle JKO$ and $m\angle KOJ < 90$

Note: Some acute, equiangular, right, and obtuse triangles can also be scalene, isosceles, and equilateral.

Set 23

State the name of the triangle based on the measures given. If the information describes a figure that cannot be a triangle, write, "Cannot be a triangle."

115. ΔBDE, where $m\overline{BD} = 17$, $m\overline{BE} = 22$, $m\angle D = 47°$, and $m\angle B = 47$.

116. ΔQRS, where $m\angle R = 94$, $m\angle Q = 22$ and $m\angle S = 90$.

117. ΔWXY, where $m\overline{WX} = 10$, $m\overline{XY} = 10$, $m\overline{YW} = 10$, and $m\angle X = 90$.

118. ΔPQR, where $m\angle P = 31$ and $m\angle R = 89$.

119. ΔABD, where $m\overline{AB} = 72$, $m\overline{AD} = 72$ and $m\angle A = 90$.

120. ΔTAR, where $m\angle 1 = 184$ and $m\angle 2 = 86$.

121. ΔDEZ, where $m\angle 1 = 60$ and $m\angle 2 = 60$.

122. ΔCHI, where $m\angle 1 = 30$, $m\angle 2 = 60$ and $m\angle 3 = 90$.

123. ΔJMR, where $m\angle 1 = 5$, $m\angle 2 = 120$ and $m\angle 3 = 67$.

124. ΔKLM, where $m\overline{KL} = m\overline{LM} = m\overline{MK}$.

Set 24

Fill in the blanks based on your knowledge of triangles and angles.

125. In right triangle ABC, if $\angle C$ measures 31° and $\angle A$ measures 90°, then $\angle B$ measures _____.

126. In scalene triangle QRS, if $\angle R$ measures 134° and $\angle Q$ measures 16°, then $\angle S$ measures _____.

127. In isosceles triangle TUV, if vertex ∠T is supplementary to an angle in an equilateral triangle, then base ∠U measures _____.

128. In obtuse isosceles triangle EFG, if the base ∠F measures 12, then the vertex ∠E measures _____.

129. In acute triangle ABC, if ∠B measures 45°, can ∠C measure 30°? _____.

Set 25

Choose the best answer.

130. Which of the following sets of interior angle measures would describe an acute isosceles triangle?
a. 90°, 45°, 45°
b. 80°, 60°, 60°
c. 60°, 60°, 60°
d. 60°, 50°, 50°

131. Which of the following sets of interior angle measures would describe an obtuse isosceles triangle?
a. 90°, 45°, 45°
b. 90°, 90°, 90°
c. 100°, 50°, 50°
d. 120°, 30°, 30°

132. Which of the following angle measurements **would not** describe an interior angle of a right angle?
a. 30°
b. 60°
c. 90°
d. 100°

133. If △JNM is equilateral and equiangular, which condition would not exist?

    a. $m\overline{JN} = m\overline{MN}$

    b. $\overline{JM} \cong \overline{JN}$

    c. $m\angle N = m\angle J$

    d. $m\angle M = m\overline{NM}$

134. In isosceles △ABC, if vertex ∠A is twice the measure of base ∠B, then ∠C measures

    a. 30°.

    b. 33°.

    c. 45°.

    d. 90°.

Set 26

Using the obtuse triangle diagram below, determine which of the pair of angles given has a greater measure. Note: $m\angle 2 = 111$.

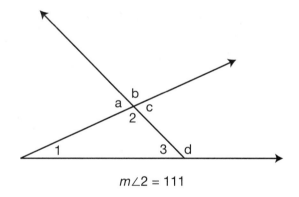

$m\angle 2 = 111$

135. ∠1 or ∠2

136. ∠3 or ∠d

137. ∠a or ∠b

138. ∠1 or ∠c

139. ∠a or ∠c

140. ∠3 or ∠b

141. ∠2 or ∠d

Answers

Set 23

115. **Isosceles triangle BDE.** Base angles D and B are congruent.

116. **Not a triangle.** Any triangle can have one right angle or one obtuse angle, not both. "Triangle" QRS claims to have a right angle and an obtuse angle.

117. **Not a triangle.** "Triangle" WXY claims to be equilateral and right; however, an equilateral triangle also has three congruent interior angles, and no triangle can have three right angles.

118. **Acute scalene triangle PQR.** Subtract from 180° the sum of ∠P and ∠R. ∠Q measures 60°. All three angles are acute, and all three angles are different. ΔPQR is acute scalene.

119. **Not a triangle.** Add the measure of each angle together. The sum of the measure of interior angles exceeds 180°.

120. **Not a triangle.** Every angle in a triangle measures less than 180°. "Triangle" TAR claims to have an angle that measures 184°.

121. **Acute equilateral triangle DEZ.** Subtract from 180° the sum of ∠1 and ∠2. ∠3, like ∠1 and ∠2, measures 60°. An equiangular triangle is an equilateral triangle, and both are always acute.

122. **Scalene right triangle CHI.** ∠3 is a right angle; ∠1 and ∠2 are acute; and all three sides have different lengths.

123. **Not a triangle.** Add the measure of each angle together. The sum of the measure of interior angles exceeds 180°.

124. **Acute equilateral triangle KLM.**

Set 24

125. **59°.** $180 - (m\angle C + m\angle A) = m\angle B$. $180 - 121 = m\angle B$. $59 = m\angle B$

126. **30°.** $180 - (m\angle R + m\angle Q) = m\angle S$. $180 - 150 = m\angle S$. $30 = m\angle S$

127. **30°.** Step One: $180 - 60 = m\angle T$. $120 = m\angle T$. Step Two: $180 - m\angle T = m\angle U + m\angle V$. $180 - 120 = m\angle U + m\angle V$. $60 = m\angle U + m\angle V$. Step Three: 60° shared by two congruent base angles equals two 30° angles.

128. **156°.** $180 - (m\angle F + m\angle G) = m\angle E$. $180 - 24 = m\angle E$. $156 = m\angle E$

129. **No.** The sum of the measures of $\angle B$ and $\angle C$ equals 75°. Subtract 75° from 180°, and $\angle A$ measures 105°. $\triangle ABC$ cannot be acute if any of its interior angles measure 90° or more.

Set 25

130. **c.** Choice **a** is not an acute triangle because it has one right angle. In choice **b**, the sum of interior angle measures exceeds 180°. Choice **d** suffers the reverse problem; its sum does not make 180°. Though choice **c** describes an equilateral triangle; it also describes an isosceles triangle.

131. **d.** Choice **a** is not an obtuse triangle; it is a right triangle. The triangle described in choice **b** does not exist. In choice **c**, the sum of the interior angle measures exceeds 180°.

132. **d.** A right triangle has a right angle and two acute angles; it does not have any obtuse angles.

133. **d.** Angles and sides are measured in different units. 60 inches is not the same as 60°.

134. **c.** Let $m\angle A = 2x$, $m\angle B = x$ and $m\angle C = x$. $2x + x + x = 180°$. $4x = 180°$. $x = 45°$.

Set 26

135. ∠2. If ∠2 is the obtuse angle in an obtuse triangle, ∠1 and ∠3 must be acute.

136. ∠d. If ∠3 is acute, its supplement is obtuse.

137. ∠b. ∠b is vertical to obtuse angle 2, which means ∠b is also obtuse. The supplement to an obtuse angle is always acute.

138. ∠c. The measure of an exterior angle equals the measure of the sum of nonadjacent interior angles, which means the measure of ∠c equals the measure of ∠1 plus the measure of ∠3. It only makes sense that the measure of ∠c is greater than the measure of ∠1 all by itself.

139. *m∠a equals m∠c.* ∠a and ∠c are a vertical pair. They are congruent and equal.

140. ∠b. ∠b is the vertical angle to obtuse ∠2, which means ∠b is also obtuse. Just as the measure of ∠2 exceeds the measure of ∠3, so too does the measure of ∠b.

141. ∠d. The measure of an exterior angle equals the measure of the sum of nonadjacent interior angles, which means the measure of ∠d equals the measure of ∠1 plus the measure of ∠2. It only makes sense that the measure of ∠d is greater than the measure of ∠2 all by itself.

7

Congruent Triangles

Look in a regular bathroom mirror and you'll see your reflection. Same shape, same size. Look at a 3 × 5 photograph of yourself. That is also you, but much smaller. Look at the people around you. Unless you have a twin, they aren't you; and they do not look anything like you. In geometry, figures also have their duplicates. Some triangles are exactly alike; some are very alike, and some are not alike at all.

Congruent Triangles

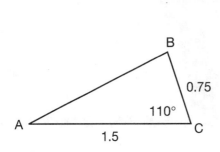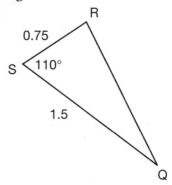

Corresponding Parts of Congruent Triangles
Are Congruent (CPCTC)

$\overline{AB} \cong \overline{RQ}$	$\angle A \cong LQ$
$\overline{BC} \cong \overline{RS}$	$\angle B \cong LR$
$\overline{CA} \cong \overline{SQ}$	$\angle C \cong LS$

Same size
Same shape
Same measurements

Similar Triangles

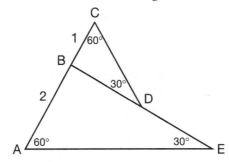

Corresponding Angles of Similar Triangles
Are Congruent (CASTC)

$\angle A \cong \angle C$
$\angle ABD \cong \angle CBD$
$\angle CBD \cong \angle AED$

Corresponding Sides of Similar Triangles
Are Proportional (CPSTP)

$2 \times \overline{BC} = 1 \times \overline{AB}$
$2 \times \overline{BD} = 1 \times \overline{BE}$
$2 \times \overline{CD} = 1 \times \overline{AE}$

Different sizes
Same shape
Different measurements, but in proportion

Dissimilar Triangles

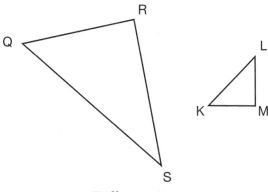

Different sizes
Different shapes
Different measurements

The ability to show two triangles are congruent or similar is useful when establishing relationships between different planar figures. This chapter focuses on proving congruent triangles using formal **postulates**—those simple reversal statements that define geometry's truths. The next chapter will look at proving similar triangles.

Congruent Triangles

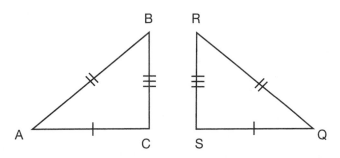

Side-Side-Side (SSS) Postulate: If three sides of one triangle are congruent to three sides of another triangle, then the two triangles are congruent.

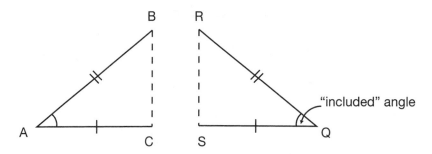

Side-Angle-Side (SAS) Postulate: If two sides and the included angle of one triangle are congruent to the corresponding parts of another triangle, then the triangles are congruent.

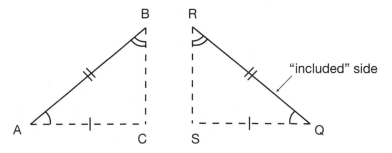

Angle-Side-Angle (ASA) Postulate: If two angles and the included side of one triangle are congruent to corresponding parts of another triangle, the triangles are congruent.

Set 27

Choose the best answer.

142. In ΔABC and ΔLMN, ∠A and ∠L are congruent, ∠B and ∠M are congruent and ∠C and ∠N are congruent. Using the information above, which postulate proves that ΔABC and ΔLMN are congruent? If congruency cannot be determined, choose choice **d.**
   a. SSS
   b. SAS
   c. ASA
   d. It cannot be determined.

143. The Springfield cheerleaders need to make three identical triangles. The girls decide to use an arm length to separate each girl from her two other squad mates. Which postulate proves that their triangles are congruent? If congruency cannot be determined, choose choice **d**.
    a. SSS
    b. SAS
    c. ASA
    d. It cannot be determined.

144. Two sets of the same book are stacked triangularly against opposite walls. Both sets must look exactly alike. They are twelve books high against the wall, and twelve books from the wall. Which postulate proves that the two stacks are congruent? If congruency cannot be determined, choose choice **d**.
    a. SSS
    b. SAS
    c. ASA
    d. It cannot be determined.

Set 28

Use the figure below to answer questions 145 through 148.

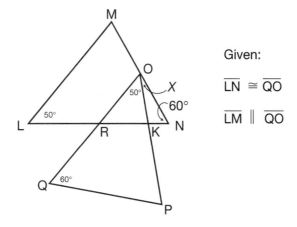

Given:

$\overline{LN} \cong \overline{QO}$

$\overline{LM} \parallel \overline{QO}$

145. Name each of the triangles in order of corresponding vertices.

146. Name corresponding line segments.

147. State the postulate that proves ΔLMN is congruent to ΔOPQ.

148. Find the measure of ∠X.

Set 29

Use the figure below to answer questions 149 through 152.

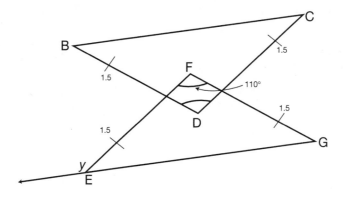

149. Name each of the triangles in order of corresponding vertices.

150. Name corresponding line segments.

151. State the postulate that proves ΔBCD is congruent to ΔEFG.

152. Find the measure of ∠y.

Set 30

Use the figure below to answer questions 153 through 156.

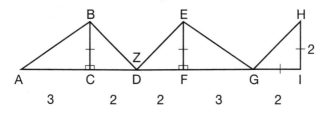

153. Name each of the triangles in order of corresponding vertices.

154. Name corresponding line segments.

155. State the postulate that proves ΔABC is congruent to ΔGEF.

156. Find the measure of ∠Z.

Set 31

Use the figure below to answer questions 157 through 160.

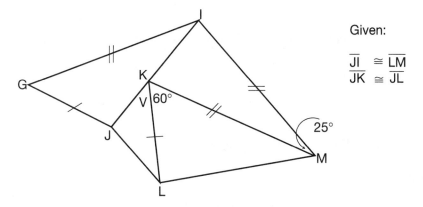

Given:

$$\overline{JI} \cong \overline{LM}$$
$$\overline{JK} \cong \overline{JL}$$

157. Name each of the triangles according to their corresponding vertices.

158. Name corresponding line segments.

159. State the postulate that proves ΔGIJ is congruent to ΔKML.

160. Find the measure of ∠V.

Set 32

Use the diagram below to answer questions 161 through 163.

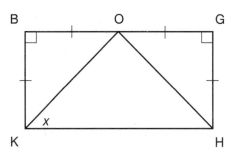

161. In the figure above, which triangles are congruent? What postulate proves it?

162. ΔHGO is a _____ triangle.

163. ∠X measures _____ degrees.

Answers

Set 27

142. **d.** Congruency cannot be determined. In later chapters you will learn more about similar triangles; but in this chapter you need to know that congruent angles are not enough to prove triangles are congruent.

143. **a.** As long as the arm lengths are consistent, there will be only one way to form those cheering triangles.

144. **b.** Do not be afraid to sketch this problem if you are having difficulty visualizing it. The wall and floor plane form a right angle. The legs of each stack measure 12 books. Both stacks are right triangles with leg lengths of 12 and 12.

Set 28

145. **ΔLMN and ΔOPQ.** (Always coordinate corresponding vertices.)

146. $\overline{LM} \cong \overline{OP}$
$\overline{MN} \cong \overline{PQ}$
$\overline{NL} \cong \overline{QO}$
(Always coordinate corresponding endpoints.)

147. **Angle-Side-Angle postulate:** $\angle N \cong \angle Q$
$\overline{LN} \cong \overline{QO}$
$\angle L \cong \angle O$

148. $x = 20$. When a transversal crosses a pair of parallel lines, corresponding angles are congruent; so, $\angle ORN$ measures 50°. $\angle OKR$ measures 80°, and $\angle OKR$'s supplement, $\angle OKN$, measures 100°. Finally, $180 - (100 + 60) = 20$.

Set 29

149. **△CDB and △EFG.** (Remember to align corresponding vertices.)

150. $\overline{CD} \cong \overline{EF}$
$\overline{DB} \cong \overline{FG}$
$\overline{BC} \cong \overline{GE}$
(Always coordinate corresponding endpoints.)

151. **Side-Angle-Side Postulate:** $\overline{BD} \cong \overline{FG}$
$\angle D \cong \angle F$
$\overline{CD} \cong \overline{EF}$

152. $m\angle Y = 145$. △EFG is an isosceles triangle whose vertex measures 110°. Both base angles measure half the difference of 110 from 180, or 35°. $m\angle Y = m\angle F + m\angle G$; $m\angle Y = 110 + 35$.

Set 30

153. **There are two sets of congruent triangles in this question.** △ABC and △GEF make one set. △DBC, △DEF, and △GHI make the second set. (Remember to align corresponding vertices.)

154. **Set one:** $\overline{AB} \cong \overline{GE}$
Set two: $\overline{DB} \cong \overline{DE} \cong \overline{GH}$
$\overline{BC} \cong \overline{EF}$ $\qquad \overline{BC} \cong \overline{EF} \cong \overline{HI}$
$\overline{CA} \cong \overline{FG}$ $\qquad \overline{DC} \cong \overline{DF} \cong \overline{GI}$
(Always coordinate corresponding endpoints.)

155. **Side-Angle-Side:**
Set one: $\overline{BC} \cong \overline{EF}$
Set two: $\overline{BC} \cong \overline{EF} \cong \overline{HI}$
$\angle BCA \cong \angle EFG$ $\quad \angle BCD \cong \angle EFD \cong \angle I$
$\overline{CA} \cong \overline{FG}$ $\qquad \overline{CD} \cong \overline{FD} \cong \overline{IG}$

156. $m\angle Z = 90°$. △DBC and △DEF are isosceles right triangles, which means the measures of $\angle BDC$ and $\angle EDF$ both equal 45°. $180 - (m\angle BDC + m\angle EDF) = m\angle Z$. $180 - 90 = m\angle Z$.

Set 31

157. ΔKML and ΔGIJ. (Remember to align corresponding vertices.)

158. $\overline{KM} \cong \overline{GI}$
$\overline{ML} \cong \overline{IJ}$
$\overline{LK} \cong \overline{JG}$
(Always coordinate corresponding endpoints.)

159. Side-Side-Side: $\overline{KM} \cong \overline{GI}$
$\overline{ML} \cong \overline{IJ}$
$\overline{LK} \cong \overline{JG}$

160. $m\angle V = 42.5°$. ΔIMK is an isosceles triangle. Its vertex angle measures 25°; its base angles measure 77.5° each. $180 - (m\angle IKM + m\angle MKL) = m\angle JKL$. $180 - (77.5 + 60) = m\angle JKL$. $m\angle JKL = 42.5$.

Set 32

161. ΔKBO and ΔHGO are congruent; Side-Angle-Side postulate.

162. isosceles right triangle

163. 45°

8

Ratio, Proportion, and Similarity

If congruent triangles are like mirrors or identical twins, then similar triangles are like fraternal twins: They are not exactly the same; however, they are very related. Similar triangles share congruent angles and congruent shapes. Only their sizes differ. So, when does size matter? In geometry, often—if it's proportional.

Similar Triangles

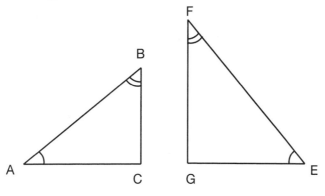

Angle-Angle (AA) Postulate: If two angles of one triangle are congruent to two angles of another triangle, then the triangles are similar.

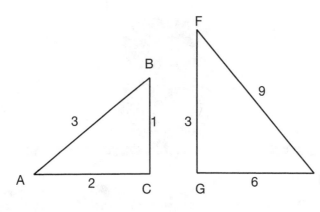

See Ratios and Proportions

$$\overline{AB} : \overline{EF} = 3:9$$

$$\overline{BC} : \overline{PG} = 1:3$$

$$\overline{CA} : \overline{GE} = 2:6$$

$$3:9 = 2:6 = 1:3$$

Reduce each ratio,

$$1:3 = 1:3 = 1:3$$

Side-Side-Side (SSS) Postulate: If the lengths of the corresponding sides of two triangles are proportional, then the triangles are similar.

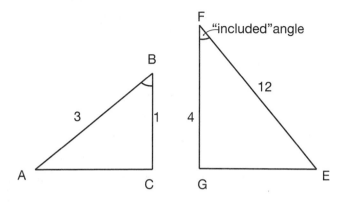

See Ratios and Proportions

$$\overline{AB} : \overline{EF} = 3:12$$

$$\overline{BC} : \overline{FG} = 1:4$$

$$3:12 = 1:4$$

Reduce each ratio,

$$1:4 = 1:4$$

Side-Angle-Side (SAS) Postulate: If the lengths of two pairs of corresponding sides of two triangles are proportional and the corresponding included angles are congruent, then the triangles are similar.

Ratios and Proportions

A **ratio** is a statement comparing any two quantities. If I have 10 bikes and you have 20 cars, then the ratio of my bikes to your cars is 10 to 20. This ratio can be simplified to 1 to 2 by dividing each side of the ratio by the greatest common factor (in this case, 10). Ratios are commonly written with a colon between the sets of objects being compared.

$$10:20$$
$$1:2$$

A **proportion** is a statement comparing two equal ratios. The ratio of my blue pens to my black pens is 7:2; I add four more black pens to my collection. How many blue pens must I add to maintain the same ratio of blue pens to black pens in my collection? The answer: 14 blue pens. Compare the ratios:

$$7:2 = 21:6,$$

If you reduce the right side, the proportion reads 7:2 = 7:2

A proportion can also be written as a fraction:

$$\frac{7}{2} = \frac{21}{6}$$

Proportions and ratios are useful for finding unknown sides of similar triangles because corresponding sides of similar triangles are always proportional.

Caution: When writing a proportion, always line up like ratios. The ratio 7:2 is not equal to the ratio 6:21!

Set 33

Choose the best answer.

164. If ΔDFG and ΔJKL are both right and isosceles, which postulate proves they are similar?
  a. Angle-Angle
  b. Side-Side-Side
  c. Side-Angle-Side
  d. Angle-Side-Angle

165. In ΔABC, side AB measures 16 inches. In similar ΔEFG, corresponding side EF measures 24 inches. State the ratio of side AB to side EF.
  a. 2:4
  b. 2:3
  c. 2:1
  d. 8:4

166. Use the figure below to find a proportion to solve for x.

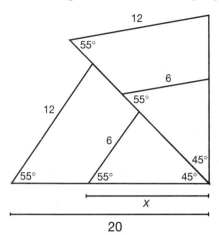

a. $\dfrac{12}{6} = \dfrac{20}{(20-x)}$

b. $\dfrac{12}{20} = \dfrac{x}{6}$

c. $\dfrac{20}{12} = \dfrac{6}{x}$

d. $\dfrac{12}{6} = \dfrac{20}{x}$

167. In similar triangles UBE and ADF, $\overline{UB}$ measures 10 inches while corresponding $\overline{AD}$ measures 2 inches. If $\overline{BE}$ measures 30 inches, then corresponding $\overline{DF}$ measures

a. 150 inches.

b. 60 inches.

c. 12 inches.

d. 6 inches.

Set 34

Use the figure below to answer questions 168 through 171.

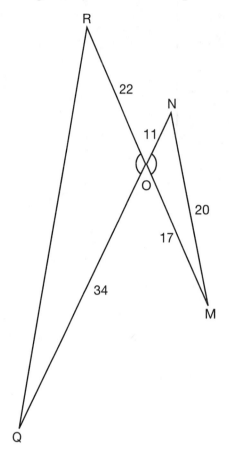

168. Name each of the triangles in order of their corresponding vertices.

169. Name corresponding line segments.

170. State the postulate that proves similarity.

171. Find $\overline{RQ}$.

Set 35

Use the figure below to answer questions 172 through 175.

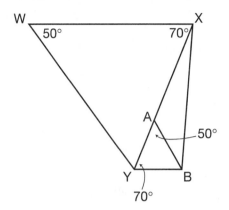

172. Name each of the triangles in order of their corresponding vertices.

173. Name corresponding line segments.

174. State the postulate that proves similarity.

175. Prove that $\overline{WX}$ and $\overline{YB}$ are parallel.

Set 36

Use the figure below to answer questions 176 through 179.

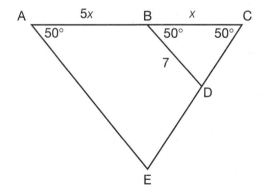

176. Name each of the triangles in order of their corresponding vertices.

177. Name corresponding line segments.

178. State the postulate that proves similarity.

179. Find $\overline{AE}$.

Set 37

Fill in the blanks with a letter from a corresponding figure in the box below.

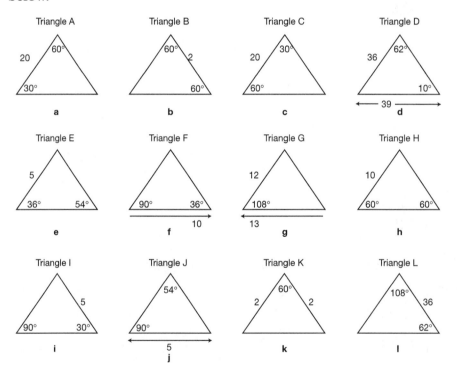

180. Choice _____ is congruent to ΔA.

181. Choice _____ is similar to ΔA.

182. Choice _____ is congruent to ΔB.

183. Choice _____ is similar to ΔB.

184. Choice _____ is congruent to ΔE.

185. Choice _____ is similar to ΔE.

186. Choice _____ is congruent to ΔD.

187. Choice _____ is similar to ΔD.

188. Triangle(s)_____ are right triangles.

189. Triangle(s)_____ are equilateral triangles.

Answers

Set 33

164. **a.** The angles of a right isosceles triangle always measure 45 – 45 – 90. Since at least two corresponding angles are congruent, right isosceles triangles are similar.

165. **b.** A ratio is a comparison. If one side of a triangle measures 16 inches, and a corresponding side in another triangle measures 24 inches, then the ratio is 16:24. This ratio can be simplified by dividing each side of the ratio by the common factor 8. The comparison now reads, 2:3 or *2 to 3*. Choices **a**, **c**, and **d** simplify into the same incorrect ratio of 2:1 or 1:2.

166. **d.** When writing a proportion, corresponding parts must parallel each other. The proportions in choices **b** and **c** are misaligned. Choice **a** looks for the line segment $20 - x$, not x.

167. **d.** First, state the ratio between similar triangles; that ratio is 10:2 or 5:1. The ratio means that a line segment in the larger triangle is always 5 times more than the corresponding line segment in a similar triangle. If the line segment measures 30 inches, it is 5 times more than the corresponding line segment. Create the equation: $30 = 5x$. $x = 6$.

Set 34

168. **△OQR and △OMN.** (Remember to align corresponding vertices.)

169. **Corresponding line segments are $\overline{OQ}$ and $\overline{OM}$; $\overline{QR}$ and $\overline{MN}$; $\overline{RO}$ and $\overline{NO}$.** Always coordinate corresponding endpoints.

170. **Side-Angle-Side.** The sides of similar triangles are not congruent; they are proportional. If the ratio between corresponding line-segments, $\overline{RO}$ and $\overline{NO}$ is 22:11, or 2:1, and the ratio between corresponding line segments $\overline{QO}$ and $\overline{MO}$ is also 2:1, they are proportional.

171. *x* **= 40.** From the last question, you know the ratio between similar triangles OQR and OMN is 2:1. That ratio means that a line segment in the smaller triangle is half the size of the corresponding line segment in the larger triangle. If that line segment measures 20 inches, it is half the size of the corresponding line segment. Create the equation: $20 = \frac{1}{2}x$. *x* = 40.

Set 35

172. **ΔWXY and ΔAYB.** (Remember to align corresponding vertices.)

173. **Corresponding line segments are $\overline{WX}$ and $\overline{AY}$; $\overline{XY}$ and $\overline{YB}$; $\overline{YW}$ and $\overline{BA}$.** Always coordinate corresponding endpoints.

174. **Angle-Angle postulate.** Since there are no side measurements to compare, only an all-angular postulate can prove triangle similarity.

175. **$\overline{XY}$ acts like a transversal across $\overline{WX}$ and $\overline{BY}$.** When alternate interior angles are congruent, then lines are parallel. In this case, ∠WXY and ∠BYA are congruent alternate interior angles. $\overline{WX}$ and $\overline{BY}$ are parallel.

Set 36

176. **ΔAEC and ΔBDC.** (Remember to align corresponding vertices.)

177. **Corresponding line segments are $\overline{AE}$ and $\overline{BD}$; $\overline{EC}$ and $\overline{DC}$; $\overline{CA}$ and $\overline{CB}$.** Always coordinate corresponding endpoints.

178. **Angle-Angle postulate.** Though it is easy to overlook, vertex C applies to both triangles.

179. *x* **= 42.** This is a little tricky. When you state the ratio between triangles, remember that corresponding sides $\overline{AC}$ and $\overline{BC}$ share part of a line segment. $\overline{AC}$ actually measures $5x + x$, or $6x$. The ratio is $6x:1x$, or 6:1. If the side of the smaller triangle measures 7, then the corresponding side of the larger triangle will measure 6 times 7, or 42.

Set 37

180. **c.** Because the two angles given in ΔA are 30° and 60°, the third angle in ΔA is 90°. Like ΔA, choices **c** and **i** also have angles that measure 30°, 60°, and 90°. According to the Angle-Angle postulate, at least two congruent angles prove similarity. To be congruent, an included side must also be congruent. ΔA and the triangle in choice **c** have congruent hypotenuses. They are congruent.

181. **i.** In the previous answer, choice **c** was determined to be congruent to ΔA because of congruent sides. In choice **i**, the triangle's hypotenuse measures 5; it has the same shape as ΔA but is smaller; consequently, they are not congruent triangles; they are only similar triangles.

182. **k.** ΔB is an equilateral triangle. Choices **h** and **k** are also equilateral triangles (an isosceles triangle whose vertex measures 60° must also have base angles that measure 60°). However, only choice **k** and ΔB are congruent because of congruent sides.

183. **h.** Choice **h** has the same equilateral shape as ΔB, but they are different sizes. They are not congruent; they are only similar.

184. **j.** The three angles in ΔE measure 36°, 54°, and 90°. Choices **f** and **j** also have angles that measure 36°, 54°, and 90°. According to the Angle-Angle postulate, at last two congruent angles prove similarity. To be congruent, an included side must also be congruent. The line segments between the 36° and 90° angles in choices **j** and **e** are congruent.

185. **f.** Choice **f** has the same right scalene shape as ΔE, but they are not congruent; they are only similar.

186. **l.** The three angles in ΔD respectively measure 62°, 10°, and 108°. Choice **l** has a set of corresponding and congruent angles, which proves similarity; but choice **l** also has an included congruent side, which proves congruency.

187. **g.** Choice **g** has only one given angle; the Side-Angle-Side postulate proves it is similar to ΔD. The sides on either side of the 108° angle are proportional and the included angle is obviously congruent.

188. **a, c, e, f, i, j.** Any triangle with a 90° interior angle is a right triangle.

189. **b, h, k.** Any triangle with congruent sides and congruent angles is an equilateral, equiangular triangle.

Triangles and the Pythagorean Theorem

In Chapters 7 and 8, you found the unknown sides of a triangle using the known sides of similar and congruent triangles. To find an unknown side of a single right triangle, you will need the Pythagorean theorem.

To use the Pythagorean theorem, you must know squares—not the four-sided figure—but a number times itself. A number multiplied by itself is *raised to the second power.*

$$4 \times 4 = 16$$

$$4^{2(\text{exponent})} (\text{base}) = 16$$

Pythagorean Theorem

$$a^2 + b^2 = c^2$$

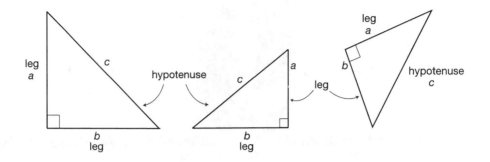

The longest side is always the hypotenuse;
therefore the longest side is always *c*.

Find hypotenuse $\overline{QR}$.

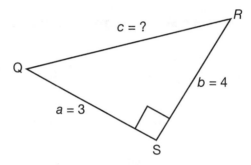

$$a^2 + b^2 = c^2$$

$$3^2 + 4^2 = c^2$$

$$9 + 16 = c^2$$

$$25 = c^2$$

Take the square root of each side:

$$\sqrt{25} = \sqrt{c^2}$$

$$5 = c$$

Find $\overline{KL}$.

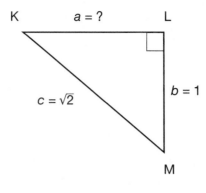

$$a^2 + b^2 = c^2$$

$$a^2 + 1^2 = \sqrt{2}^2$$

$$a^2 + 1 = 2$$

$$a^2 = 1$$

Take the square root of each side:

$$\sqrt{a^2} = \sqrt{1}$$

Find $\overline{CD}$.

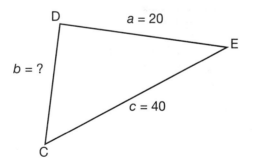

$$a^2 + b^2 = c^2$$

$$20^2 + b^2 = 40^2$$

$$400 + b^2 = 1,600$$

$$b^2 = 1,200$$

Take the square root of each side:

$$\sqrt{b^2} = \sqrt{1,200}$$

$$b = 20\sqrt{3}$$

The Pythagorean theorem can only find a side of a right triangle. However, if all the sides of any given triangle are known, but none of the angles are known, the Pythagorean theorem can tell you whether that triangle is obtuse or acute.

Is △GHI obtuse or acute?

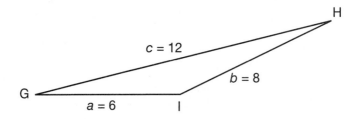

$a^2 + b^2$	c^2
$6^2 + 8^2$	12^2
$36 + 64$	144

100   <   144,

Therefore, △GHI is obtuse.

Is △JKL obtuse or acute?

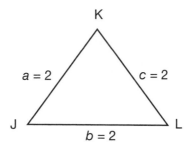

$a^2 + b^2$	c^2
$2^2 + 2^2$	2^2
$4 + 4$	4

8   >   4

Therefore, △JKL is acute.

Set 38

Choose the best answer.

190. If the sides of a triangle measure 3, 4, and 5, then the triangle is
    a. acute.
    b. right.
    c. obtuse.
    d. It cannot be determined.

191. If the sides of a triangle measure 12, 16, and 20, then the triangle is
    a. acute.
    b. right.
    c. obtuse.
    d. It cannot be determined.

192. If the sides of a triangle measure 15, 17, and 22, then the triangle is
   a. acute.
   b. right.
   c. obtuse.
   d. It cannot be determined.

193. If the sides of a triangle measure 6, 16, and 26, then the triangle is
   a. acute.
   b. right.
   c. obtuse.
   d. It cannot be determined.

194. If the sides of a triangle measure 12, 12, and 15, then the triangle is
   a. acute.
   b. right.
   c. obtuse.
   d. It cannot be determined.

195. If two sides of a triangle measure 4 and 14, and an angle measures 34°, then the triangle is
   a. acute.
   b. right.
   c. obtuse.
   d. It cannot be determined.

196. If the sides of a triangle measure 2, 3, and 16, then the triangle is
   a. acute.
   b. right.
   c. obtuse.
   d. It cannot be determined.

Set 39

Choose the best answer.

197. Eva and Carr meet at a corner. Eva turns 90° left and walks 5 paces; Carr continues straight and walks 6 paces. If a line segment connected them, it would measure
a. $\sqrt{22}$ paces.
b. $\sqrt{25}$ paces.
c. $\sqrt{36}$ paces.
d. $\sqrt{61}$ paces.

198. The legs of a table measure 3 feet long and the top measures 4 feet long. If the legs are connected to the table at a right angle, then what is the distance between the bottom of each leg and the end of the tabletop?
a. 5 feet
b. 7 feet
c. 14 feet
d. 25 feet

199. Dorothy is standing directly 300 meters under a plane. She sees another plane flying straight behind the first. It is 500 meters away from her, and she has not moved. How far apart are the planes from each other?
a. 40 meters
b. 400 meters
c. 4,000 meters
d. 40,000 meters

200. Timmy arranges the walls of his shed on the ground. The base of the first side measures 10 feet. The base of the second side measures 15 feet. If the walls are at a right angle from each other, the measure from the end of one side to the end of the second side equals
a. 35 feet.
b. 50 feet.
c. $\sqrt{225}$ feet.
d. $\sqrt{325}$ feet.

Set 40

Use the figure below to answer questions 201 through 203.

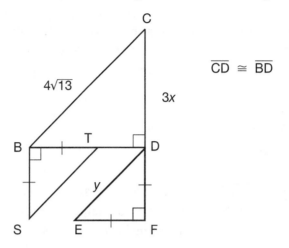

$\overline{CD} \cong \overline{BD}$

201. Which triangles in the figure above are congruent and/or similar?

202. Find the value of x.

203. Find the value of y.

Set 41

Use the figure below to answer questions 204 through 206.

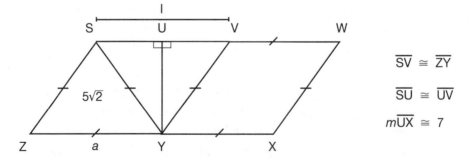

$\overline{SV} \cong \overline{ZY}$

$\overline{SU} \cong \overline{UV}$

$m\overline{UX} \cong 7$

204. Which triangles in the figure above are congruent and/or similar?

205. Find the value of a.

206. Is $\triangle ZSY$ acute or obtuse?

Set 42

Use the figure below to answer questions 207 through 209.

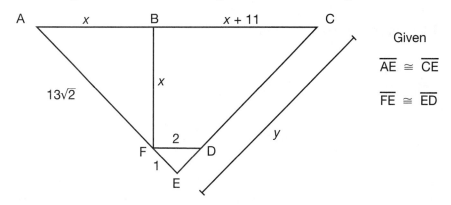

Given

$\overline{AE} \cong \overline{CE}$

$\overline{FE} \cong \overline{ED}$

207. Which triangles in the figure above are congruent and/or similar?

208. Find the value of x.

209. Find the value of y.

Set 43

Use the figure below to answer questions 210 through 215.

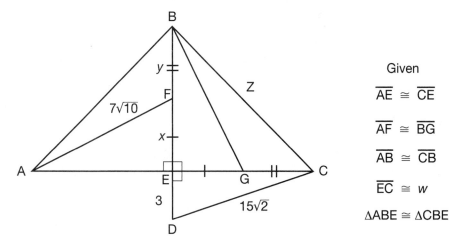

Given

$\overline{AE} \cong \overline{CE}$

$\overline{AF} \cong \overline{BG}$

$\overline{AB} \cong \overline{CB}$

$\overline{EC} \cong w$

$\triangle ABE \cong \triangle CBE$

210. Which triangles in the figure above are congruent and/or similar?

211. Find the value of w.

212. Find the value of x.

213. Find the value of y.

214. Find the value of Z.

215. Is $\triangle$BGC acute or obtuse?

Answers

Set 38

190. **b.** This is a popular triangle, so know it well. A 3-4-5 triangle is a right triangle. Apply the Pythagorean theorem: $a^2 + b^2 = c^2$. $3^2 + 4^2 = 5^2$. $9 + 16 = 25$. $25 = 25$.

191. **b.** This is also a 3–4–5 triangle. Simplify the measurement of each side by dividing 12, 16, and 20 by 4: $\frac{12}{4} = 3$. $\frac{16}{4} = 4$. $\frac{20}{4} = 5$.

192. **a.** Plug the given measurements into the Pythagorean theorem (the largest side is always c in the theorem): $15^2 + 17^2 = 22^2$. $225 + 289 = 484$. $514 > 484$. When the sum of the smaller sides squared is greater than the square of the largest side, then the triangle is acute.

193. **c.** Plug the given measurements into the Pythagorean theorem: $6^2 + 16^2 = 26^2$. $36 + 256 = 676$. $292 < 676$. When the sum of the smaller sides squared is less than the square of the largest side, then the triangle is obtuse.

194. **a.** Plug the given measurements into the Pythagorean theorem: $12^2 + 12^2 = 15^2$. $144 + 144 = 225$. $288 > 225$. Acute.

195. **d.** The Pythagorean theorem does not include any angles. Without a third side or a definite right angle, this triangle cannot be determined.

196. **c.** Plug the given measurements into the Pythagorean theorem: $2^2 + 3^2 = 16^2$. $4 + 9 = 256$. $13 < 256$. Obtuse.

197. **d.** The corner forms the right angle of this triangle; Eva and Carr walk the distance of each leg, and the question wants to know the hypotenuse. Plug the known measurements into the Pythagorean theorem: $5^2 + 6^2 = c^2$. $25 + 36 = c^2$. $61 = c^2$. $61 = c$.

198. **a.** The connection between the leg and the tabletop forms the right angle of this triangle. The length of the leg and the length of the top are the legs of the triangle, and the question wants to know the distance of the hypotenuse. Plug the known measurements into the Pythagorean theorem: $3^2 + 4^2 = c^2$. $9 + 16 = c^2$. $25 = c^2$. $5 = c$. If you chose answer **d**, you forgot to take the square root of the 25. If you chose answer **b**, you added the legs together without squaring them first.

199. **b.** The first plane is actually this triangle's right vertex. The distance between Dorothy and the second plane is the hypotenuse. Plug the known measurements into the Pythagorean theorem: $300^2 + b^2 = 500^2$. $90,000 + b^2 = 250,000$. $b^2 = 160,000$. $b = 400$. Notice that if you divided each side by 100, this is another 3-4-5 triangle.

200. **d.** The bases of Timmy's walls form the legs of this right triangle. The hypotenuse is unknown. Plug the known measurements into the Pythagorean theorem: $10^2 + 15^2 = c^2$. $100 + 225 = c^2$. $325 = c^2$. $\sqrt{325} = c$.

Set 40

201. **$\triangle$SBT and $\triangle$EFD are congruent to each other (Side-Angle-Side theorem) and similar to $\triangle$BDC (Angle-Angle theorem).**

202. $x = 4$. Because $\triangle BCD$ is an isosceles right triangle, $\overline{BD}$ is congruent to $\overline{CD}$. Plug $3x$, $3x$, and $4\sqrt{13}$ into the Pythagorean theorem: $(3x)^2 + (3x)^2 = (4\sqrt{13})^2$. $9x^2 + 9x^2 = 288$. $18x^2 = 288$. $x^2 = 16$. $x = 4$.

203. $y = 4\sqrt{2}$. In the question above, you found x equaled 4. Plug 4, 4, and y into the Pythagorean theorem: $4^2 + 4^2 = y^2$. $16 + 16 = y^2$. $32 = y^2$. $4\sqrt{2} = y$.

Set 41

204. ΔSUY is congruent to ΔVUY (Side-Side-Side theorem).

205. $a = 2$. $m\overline{SU} + m\overline{UV} = m\overline{ZY}$. $m\overline{SU} = m\overline{UV}$. To find the measure of $\overline{SU}$, plug the given measurements of ΔSUY into the Pythagorean theorem. $7^2 + b^2 = 5\sqrt{2}$. $49 + b^2 = 50$. $b^2 = 1$. $b = \sqrt{1}$. $a = 1 + 1$.

206. Acute. ΔZSY is an isosceles triangle. Two of its sides measure $5\sqrt{2}$. The third side measures 2. Plug the given measures into the Pythagorean theorem. $(5\sqrt{2})^2 + (5\sqrt{2})^2 = 2^2$. $50 + 50 = 4$. $100 > 4$. Therefore, ΔZSY is acute.

Set 42

207. ΔACE is similar to ΔFDE (Angle-Angle theorem). Both triangles are isosceles, and they share a common vertex point. Ultimately, all their angles are congruent.

208. $x = 13$. Even though you don't know the measurement of x in ΔABF, you do know that two sides measure x. Plug the measurements of ΔABF into the Pythagorean theorem. $x^2 + x^2 = (13\sqrt{2})^2$. $2x^2 = 338$. $x^2 = 169$. $x = 13$.

209. $y = 18.5$. Plug 13 into x, and add $\overline{AB}$ and $\overline{BC}$ together: $13 + 13 + 11 = 37$. The ratio between corresponding line segments $\overline{AC}$ and $\overline{FD}$ is 37:2, or 18.5:1. If $\overline{ED}$ measures 1 (an isosceles triangle), then $\overline{EC}$ is 18.5.

Set 43

210. ΔAFE and ΔBGE are congruent (Side-Side-Side postulate). ΔABF and ΔBCG are congruent (Side-Angle-Side postulate).

211. $w = 21$. Plug the measurements of ΔECD into the Pythagorean theorem: $3^2 + w^2 = (15\sqrt{2})^2$. $9 + w^2 = 450$. $w^2 = 441$. $w = 21$.

212. $x = 7$. Corresponding parts of congruent triangles are congruent (CPCTC). If $\overline{EC}$ is 21, then $\overline{EA}$ is also 21. Plug the measurements of $\triangle AFE$ into the Pythagorean theorem: $21^2 + x^2 = (7\sqrt{10})^2$. $441 + x^2 = 490$. $x^2 = 49$. $x = 7$.

213. $y = 14$. Because of CPCTC, $\overline{AE}$ is also congruent to $\overline{BE}$. If $\overline{BE}$ is 21 and $\overline{FE}$ is 7, subtract 7 from 21 to find $\overline{BF}$. $21 - 7 = 14$.

214. $Z = 21\sqrt{2}$. Plug the measurements of $\triangle BEC$ into the Pythagorean theorem: $21^2 + 21^2 = Z^2$. $441 + 441 = Z^2$. $882 = Z^2$. $21\sqrt{2} = Z$.

215. **Obtuse.** You could just look at $\triangle BGC$ and guess that its measure exceeds 180°. However, the question wants you to apply the Pythagorean theorem: $(7\sqrt{10})^2 + 7^2 = (21\sqrt{2})^2$. $490 + 49 = 882$. $539 < 882$. $\triangle BGC$ is obtuse.

10

Properties of Polygons

A triangle has three sides and three vertices. As a rule, there is a vertex for every side of a polygon. **Consecutive sides** are adjoining sides of a polygon, and **consecutive vertices** are vertices that are at opposite ends of a side:

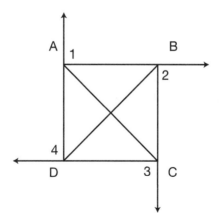

sides: $\overline{AB}$, $\overline{BC}$, $\overline{CD}$, $\overline{DA}$

vertices: ∠DAB, ∠ABC, ∠BCD, ∠CDA

interior ∠'s: DAB, ABC, BCD, CDA

exterior ∠'s: 1, 2, 3, 4

diagonals: $\overline{AC}$, $\overline{BD}$

Naming Polygons

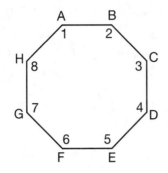

Regular Octagon ABCDEFGH

sides: $\overline{AB} \cong \overline{BC} \cong \overline{CD} \cong \overline{DE} \cong \overline{EF} \cong \overline{FG} \cong \overline{GH} \cong \overline{HA}$
interior ∠'s: $\angle 1 \cong \angle 2 \cong \angle 3 \cong \angle 4 \cong \angle 5 \cong \angle 6 \cong \angle 7 \cong \angle 8$

Regular polygons are polygons that are equilateral and equiangular.

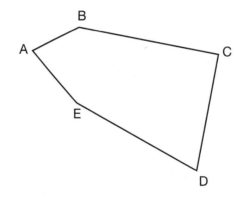

$m\angle A$, $\angle B$, $\angle C$, $\angle D$, $\angle E$, < 180,
therefore polygon ABCDE is convex.

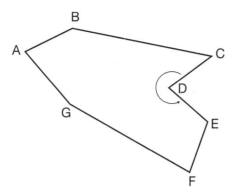

$m\angle D > 180°$, therefore polygon ABCDEFG is concave.

Vertices of a **convex polygon** all point outwards (all regular polygons are also convex polygons). If any of the vertices of a polygon point inward or if the measure of any vertex exceeds 180°, the polygon is a **concave polygon**.

Count the polygon's sides. A three-sided figure is a **triangle**. A four-sided figure is a **quadrilateral**. Five-sided figures or more take special prefixes:

Five-sided	PENTAgon
Six-sided	HEXAgon
Seven-sided	HEPTAgon
Eight-sided	OCTAgon
Nine-sided	NONAgon
Ten-sided	DECAgon
Twelve-sided	DODECAgon

SET 44

State whether the object is or is not a polygon and why. (Envision each of these objects as simply as possible, otherwise there will always be exceptions.)

216. a rectangular city block

217. Manhattan's grid of city blocks

218. branches of a tree

219. the block letter "M" carved into the tree

220. outline of a television

221. a human face on the TV

222. an ergonomic chair

223. lace

Set 45

Use the diagram below to answer questions 224 through 226.

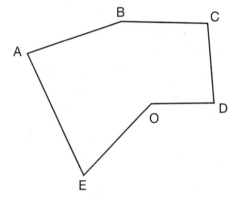

224. Name the polygon. Is it convex or concave?

225. How many diagonals can be drawn from vertex O?

226. How many sides does the polygon have? Based on its number of sides, this polygon is a _____.

Set 46

Use the diagram below to answer questions 227 through 229.

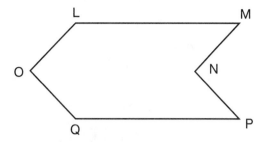

227. Name the polygon. Is it convex or concave?

228. How many diagonals can be drawn from vertex O?

229. How many sides does the polygon have? Based on its number of sides, this polygon is a _____.

Set 47

Use the diagram below to answer questions 230 through 232.

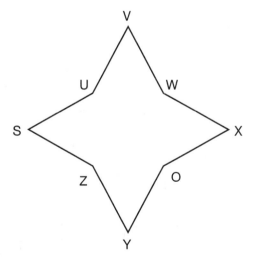

230. Name the polygon. Is it convex or concave?

231. How many diagonals can be drawn from vertex O?

232. How many sides does the polygon have? Based on its number of sides, this polygon is a _____.

Set 48

Use the diagram below to answer questions 233 through 235.

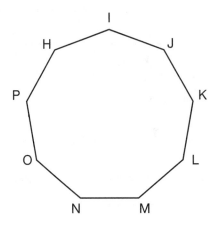

233. Name the polygon. Is it convex or concave?

234. How many diagonals can be drawn from vertex O?

235. How many sides does the polygon have? Based on its number of sides, this polygon is a _____.

Set 49

Use your knowledge of polygons to fill in the blank.

236. In polygon CDEFG, $\overline{CD}$ and $\overline{DE}$ are _____.

237. In polygon CDEFG, $\overline{CE}$, $\overline{DF}$ and $\overline{EG}$ are _____.

238. In polygon CDEFG, ∠EFG is also _____.

239. In polygon CDEFG, ∠DEF and ∠EFG are _____.

Set 50

Use diagonals to draw the triangles below.

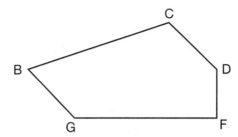

240. How many triangles can be drawn in the accompanying polygon at one time?

241. Determine the sum of the polygon's interior angles using the number of triangles; verify your answer by using the formula $s = 180(n - 2)$, where s is the sum of the interior angles and n is the number of sides the polygon has.

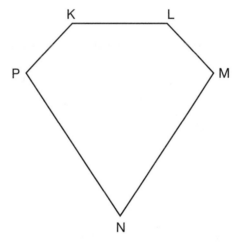

242. How many triangles can be drawn in the accompanying polygon at one time?

243. Determine the sum of the polygon's interior angles using the number of triangles; then apply the formula $s = 180 (n - 2)$ to verify your answer.

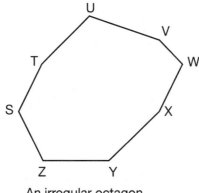

An irregular octagon

244. How many triangles can be drawn in the accompanying polygon at one time?

245. Determine the sum of the polygon's interior angles using the number of triangles; then apply the formula $s = 180 (n - 2)$ to verify your answer.

Answers

Set 44

216. **Polygon.** A single city block is a closed four-sided figure; each of its corners is a vertex.

217. **Not a polygon.** A grid is not a polygon because its lines intersect at points that are not endpoints.

218. **Not a polygon.** Branches are open, and they "branch" out at points that are also not endpoints.

219. **Polygon.** Block letters are closed multi-sided figures; each of its line segments begin and end at an endpoint.

220. **Polygon.** A classic television screen is rectangular; it has four sides and four vertices.

221. **Not a polygon.** The human face is very complex, but primarily it has few if any straight line segments.

222. **Not a polygon.** An ergonomic chair is a chair designed to contour to your body. It is usually curved to support the natural curves of the hip and spine.

223. **Not a polygon.** Like the human face, lace is very intricate. Unlike the human face, lace has lots of line segments that meet at lots of different points.

Set 45

224. **Polygon ABCDOE.** As long as you list the vertices in consecutive order, any one of these names will do: BCDOEA, CDOEAB, DOEABC, OEABCD, EABCDO. **Also, polygon ABCDOE is concave because the measure of vertex O exceeds 180°.**

225. **Three diagonals can be drawn from vertex O: $\overline{OA}$, $\overline{OB}$, $\overline{OC}$. $\overline{OD}$ and $\overline{OE}$ are not diagonals; they are sides.**

226. Polygon ABCOE has six sides; it is a hexagon.

Set 46

227. Polygon OLMNPQ. As long as you list their vertices in consecutive order, any one of these names will do: LMNPQO, MNPQOL, NPQOLM, PQOLMN, QOLMNP. **Also, polygon OLMNPQ is concave because vertex N exceeds 180°.**

228. Three diagonals can be drawn from vertex O: $\overline{OM}$, $\overline{ON}$, $\overline{OP}$.

229. Polygon OLMNPQ has 6 sides; it is a hexagon.

Set 47

230. Polygon SUVWXOYZ. If you list every vertex in consecutive order, then your name for the polygon given is correct. **Also, polygon SUVWXOYZ is concave.** The measures of vertices U, W, O and Z exceed 180°.

231. Five diagonals can be drawn from vertex O: $\overline{OZ}$, $\overline{OS}$, $\overline{OU}$, $\overline{OV}$, $\overline{OW}$.

232. Polygon SUVWXOYZ has eight sides; it is an octagon.

Set 48

233. Polygon HIJKLMNOP. List every vertex in consecutive order and your answer is correct. **Also, polygon HIJKLMNOP is regular and convex.**

234. Six diagonals can be drawn from vertex O: $\overline{OH}$, $\overline{OI}$, $\overline{OJ}$, $\overline{OK}$, $\overline{OL}$, and $\overline{OM}$.

235. Polygon HIJKLMNOP has nine sides; it is a nonagon.

Set 49

236. Consecutive sides. Draw polygon CDEFG to see that yes, $\overline{CD}$ and $\overline{DE}$ are consecutive sides.

237. Diagonals. When a line segment connects nonconsecutive endpoints in a polygon, it is a diagonal.

238. ∠GFE or ∠F.

239. Consecutive vertices. Look back at the drawing you made of polygon CDEFG. You can see that ∠E and ∠F are consecutive vertices.

Set 50

For solutions to 240 and 241, refer to image below.

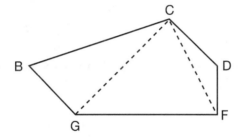

240. At any one time, three triangles can be drawn in polygon BCDFG. Remember when drawing your triangles that a diagonal must go from endpoint to endpoint.

241. The interior angles of a convex pentagon will always measure 540° together. If the interior angles of a triangle measure 180° together, then three sets of interior angles measure 180×3, or 540. Apply the formula $s = 180\,(n - 2)$. $s = 180(5 - 2)$. $s = 180(3)$. $s = 540$.

For solutions to 242 and 243, refer to the image below.

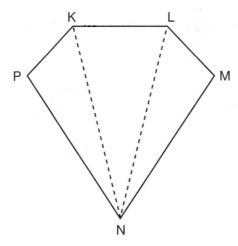

242. At any one time, three triangles can be drawn in polygon KLMNP.

243. **180 × 3 = 540.** Apply the formula $s = 180(n - 2)$. Again, $s = 540$. You have again confirmed that the interior angles of a convex pentagon will always measure 540° together.

For solutions to 244 and 245, refer to the image below.

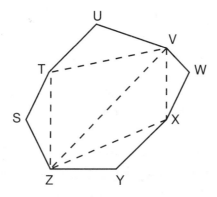

244. At any one time, six triangles can be drawn in polygon STUVWXYZ.

245. **180 × 6 = 1080.** Apply the formula $s = 180(n - 2)$. $s = 180(8 - 2)$. $s = 180(6)$. $s = 1,080$.

11

Quadrilaterals

As you would guess, triangles are not squares. Neither are parallelograms, rectangles, or rhombuses. But squares are rhombuses, rectangles, and parallelograms. How can this be?

Parallelograms, rectangles, rhombuses, and squares are all members of a four-sided polygon family called the quadrilaterals. Each member has a unique property that makes it distinctive from its fellow members. A square shares all those unique properties, making it the most unique quadrilateral.

Below are those particular characteristics that make each quadrilateral an individual.

Quadrilateral	Four-sided figure
Parallelogram	Four-sided figure
	Two pairs of parallel lines
	Opposite sides are congruent
	Opposite angles are congruent
	Consecutive angles are supplementary
	Diagonals bisect each other
Rectangle	Four-sided figure
	Two pairs of parallel lines
	Opposite sides are congruent
	All angles are congruent
	Consecutive angles are supplementary
	Diagonals bisect each other
	Diagonals are congruent

Rhombus	Four-sided figure
	Two pairs of parallel lines
	All sides are congruent
	Opposite angles are congruent
	Consecutive angles are supplementary
	Diagonals bisect each other
	Diagonals bisect the angle of a rhombus
	Diagonals form perpendicular lines
Square	Four-sided figure
	Two pairs of parallel lines
	All sides are congruent
	All angles are congruent
	Consecutive angles are supplementary
	Diagonals bisect each other
	Diagonals are congruent
	Diagonals bisect the angle of a square
	Diagonals form perpendicular lines
Trapezoid	*Four-sided figure*
	One pair of parallel lines
Isosceles Trapezoid	Four-sided figure
	One pair of parallel lines
	Congruent legs

Set 51

Choose the best answer.

246. The sides of Mary's chalkboard consecutively measure 9 feet, 5 feet, 9 feet and 5 feet. Without any other information, you can determine that Mary's chalkboard is a
   a. rectangle.
   b. rhombus.
   c. parallelogram.
   d. square.

247. Four line segments connected end-to-end will always form
   a. an open figure.
   b. four interior angles that measure 360°.
   c. a square.
   d. It cannot be determined.

248. A square whose vertices are the midpoints of another square is
   a. congruent to the other square.
   b. half the size of the other square.
   c. twice the size of the other square.
   d. It cannot be determined.

249. The sides of a square measure 2.5 feet each. If three squares fit perfectly side-by-side in one rectangle, what are the minimum dimensions of the rectangle?
   a. 5 feet, 2.5 feet, 5 feet, and 2.5 feet
   b. 7.5 feet, 7.5 feet, 7.5 feet, 7.5 feet
   c. 7.5 feet, 3 feet, 7.5 feet, 3 feet
   d. 7.5 feet, 2.5 feet, 7.5 feet, 2.5 feet

250. A rhombus, a rectangle, and an isosceles trapezoid all have
   a. congruent diagonals.
   b. opposite congruent sides.
   c. interior angles that measure 360°.
   d. opposite congruent angles.

251. A figure with four sides and four congruent angles could be a
   a. rhombus or square.
   b. rectangle or square.
   c. trapezoid or rhombus.
   d. rectangle or trapezoid.

252. A figure with four sides and perpendicular diagonals could be a
   a. rhombus or square.
   b. rectangle or square.
   c. trapezoid or rhombus.
   d. rectangle or trapezoid.

253. A figure with four sides and diagonals that bisect each angle such that each new angle is congruent could be a
   a. rectangle.
   b. rhombus.
   c. parallelogram.
   d. trapezoid.

254. A figure with four sides and diagonals that bisect each other could NOT be a
   a. rectangle.
   b. rhombus.
   c. parallelogram.
   d. trapezoid.

Set 52

Fill in the blanks based on your knowledge of quadrilaterals. More than one answer may be correct.

255. If quadrilateral ABCD has two sets of parallel lines, it could be _____.

256. If quadrilateral ABCD has four congruent sides, it could be _____.

257. If quadrilateral ABCD has exactly one set of opposite congruent sides, it could be _____.

258. If quadrilateral ABCD has opposite congruent angles, it could be _____.

259. If quadrilateral ABCD has consecutive angles that are supplementary, it could be _____.

260. If quadrilateral ABCD has congruent diagonals, it could be _____.

261. If quadrilateral ABCD can be divided into two congruent triangles, it could be _____.

262. If quadrilateral ABCD has diagonals that bisect each vertex angle in two congruent angles, it is _____.

Set 53

Choose the best answer.

263. If an angle in a rhombus measures 21°, then the other three angles consecutively measure
   a. 159°, 21°, 159°
   b. 21°, 159°, 159°
   c. 69°, 21°, 69°
   d. 21°, 69°, 69°
   e. It cannot be determined.

264. In an isosceles trapezoid, the angle opposite an angle that measures 62° measures
   a. 62°.
   b. 28°.
   c. 118°.
   d. 180°.
   e. It cannot be determined.

265. In rectangle WXYZ, ∠WXZ and ∠XZY
   a. are congruent.
   b. are alternate interior angles.
   c. form complementary angles with ∠WZX and ∠YXZ.
   d. all of the above
   e. It cannot be determined.

266. In square ABCD, ∠ABD
   a. measures 45°.
   b. is congruent with ∠ADC.
   c. forms a supplementary pair with ∠ADB.
   d. all of the above
   e. It cannot be determined.

267. In parallelogram KLMN, if diagonal KM measures 30 inches, then
   a. $\overline{KL}$ measures 18 inches.
   b. $\overline{LM}$ measures 24 inches.
   c. diagonal LN is perpendicular to diagonal KM.
   d. all of the above
   e. It cannot be determined.

Set 54

Use the figure below to answer questions 268 through 270.

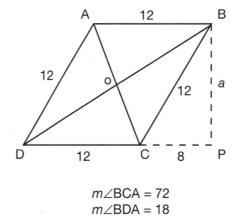

$$m\angle BCA = 72$$
$$m\angle BDA = 18$$

268. Using your knowledge of triangles and quadrilaterals, show that diagonals AC and BD intersect perpendicularly.

269. Using your knowledge of triangles and quadrilaterals, what is the length of imaginary side BP?

270. Using your knowledge of triangles and quadrilaterals, what is the length of diagonal DB?

Answers

Set 51

246. **c.** All parallelograms have opposite congruent sides including rectangles, rhombuses and squares. However, without more information, you cannot be any more specific than a parallelogram.

247. **b.** The interior angles of a quadrilateral total 360°. Choices **a** and **c** are incorrect because the question states each line segment connects end-to-end; this is a closed figure, but it is not necessarily a square.

248. **b.** Find the point along a line segment that would divide that line segment into two equal pieces. That is the line segment's midpoint. Connect the midpoint of a square together and you have another square that is half the existing square.

249. **d.** Three squares in a row will have three times the length of one square, or 2.5 in. × 3 = 7.5 in. However, the width will remain the length of just one square, or 2.5 in.

250. **c.** Rectangles and rhombuses have very little in common with isosceles trapezoids except one set of parallel lines, one set of opposite congruent sides, and four interior angles that measure 360°.

251. **b.** Rectangles and squares have four 90° angles because their four sides are perpendicular. Choices **a**, **c**, and **d** are all quadrilaterals, but they are not defined by their right angles.

252. **a.** Rhombuses and squares have congruent sides and diagonals that are perpendicular. Because their sides are not congruent, rectangles and trapezoids do not have diagonals that cross perpendicularly.

253. **b.** A rhombus's diagonal bisects its vertices.

254. **d.** Diagonals of a trapezoid are not congruent unless the trapezoid is an isosceles trapezoid. Diagonals of any trapezoid do not bisect each other.

Set 52

255. **A parallelogram, a rectangle, a rhombus, or a square.** Two pairs of parallel lines define each of these four-sided figures.

256. **a rhombus or a square**

257. **an isosceles trapezoid**

258. **A parallelogram, a rectangle, a rhombus, or a square.** When a transversal crosses a pair of parallel lines, alternate interior angles are congruent, while same side interior angles are supplementary. Draw a parallelogram, a rectangle, a rhombus, and a square; extend each of their sides. Find the "Z" and "C" shaped intersections in each drawing.

259. **A parallelogram, a rectangle, a rhombus, or a square.** Again, look at the drawing you made above to see why consecutive angles are supplementary.

260. **a rectangle or a square**

261. **all types of parallelograms and an isosceles trapezoid**

262. **a rhombus or a square**

Set 53

263. **a.** The first consecutive angle must be supplementary to the given angle. The angle opposite the given angle must be congruent. Consequently, in consecutive order, the angles measure $180 - 21$, or 159, 21, and 159. Choice **b** does not align the angles in consecutive order; choice **c** mistakenly subtracts 21 from 90 when consecutive angles are supplementary, not complementary.

264. **c.** Opposite angles in an isosceles trapezoid are supplementary. Choice **a** describes a consecutive angle along the same parallel line.

265. **d.** $\overline{XZ}$ is a diagonal in rectangle WXYZ. $\angle WXZ$ and $\angle XYZ$ are alternate interior angles along the diagonal; they are congruent; and when they are added with their adjacent angle, the two angles form a 90° angle.

266. **a.** $\overline{BD}$ is a diagonal in square ABCD. It bisects vertices B and D, creating four congruent 45° angles. Choice **b** is incorrect because $\angle ABD$ is half of $\angle ADC$; they are not congruent. Also, choice **c** is incorrect because when two 45° angles are added together they measure 90°, not 180°.

267. **e.** It cannot be determined.

Set 54

268. **Because AC and DB are intersecting straight lines, if one angle of intersection measures 90°, all four angles of intersection measure 90°, which means the lines perpendicularly meet.** First, opposite sides of a rhombus are parallel, which means alternate interior angles are congruent. If $\angle BCA$ measures 72°, then $\angle CAD$ also measures 72°. The sum of the measures of all three interior angles of a triangle must equal 180°: $72 + 28 + m\angle ADB = 180$. $m\angle AOD = 90$.

269. $a = 4\sqrt{5}$. $\overline{BP}$ is the height of rhombus ABCD and the leg of $\triangle BPC$. Use the Pythagorean theorem: $a^2 + 8^2 = 12^2$. $a^2 + 64 = 144$. $a^2 = 80$. $a = 4\sqrt{5}$.

270. $c = 4\sqrt{30}$. Use the Pythagorean theorem to find the hypotenuse of $\triangle BPD$, which is diagonal BD: $(4\sqrt{5})^2 + (12 + 8)^2 = c^2$. $80 + 400 = c^2$. $480 = c^2$. $4\sqrt{30} = c$.

12

Perimeter of Polygons

The perimeter of a figure is its outside edge, its outline. To find the perimeter of a figure, you add the length of each of its sides together.

Regular polygons use a formula: $p = ns$, where p is the polygon's perimeter; n is its number of sides; and s is the length of each side.

Set 55

Choose the best answer.

271. A regular octagonal gazebo is added to a Victorian lawn garden. Each side of the octagon measures 5 ft. The formula for the gazebo's perimeter is
   a. $p = 8 \times 5$.
   b. $8 = n \times 5$.
   c. $5 = n \times 8$.
   d. $s = n \times p$.

272. Timmy randomly walks ten steps to the left. He does this nine more times. His path never crosses itself, and he returns to his starting point. The perimeter of the figure Timmy walked equals
a. 90 steps.
b. 90 feet.
c. 100 steps.
d. 100 feet.

273. The perimeter of Periwinkle High is 1,600 ft. It has four sides of equal length. Each side measures
a. 4 ft.
b. 40 ft.
c. 400 ft.
d. 4,000 ft.

274. Roberta draws two similar pentagons. The perimeter of the larger pentagon is 93 ft.; one of its sides measures 24 ft. If the perimeter of the smaller pentagon equals 31 ft., then the corresponding side of the smaller pentagon measures
a. $5s = 31$.
b. $93s = 24 \times 31$.
c. $93 \times 24 = 31s$.
d. $5 \times 31 = s$.

275. Isadora wants to know the perimeter of the face of a building; however, she does not have a ladder. She knows that the building's rectangular facade casts a 36 ft. shadow at noon while a nearby mailbox casts a 12 ft. shadow at noon. The mailbox is 4.5 ft. tall. If the length of the façade is 54 ft. long, the façade's perimeter measures
a. $p = 13.5 \times 4$.
b. $p = 54 \times 4$.
c. $p = 4.5(2) + 12(2)$.
d. $p = 13.5(2) + 54(2)$.

Set 56

Choose the best answer.

276. Which perimeter is not the same?

a.

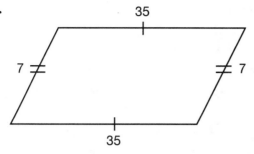

b.

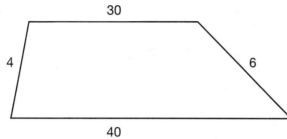

c.

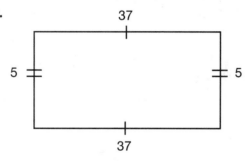

d.

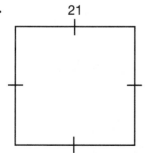

277. Which perimeter is not the same?

    a. a 12-foot regular square backyard

    b. an 8-foot regular hexagon pool

    c. a 6-foot regular octagonal patio

    d. a 4-foot regular decagon Jacuzzi

    e. It cannot be determined.

278. Which choice below has a different perimeter than the others?

    a.

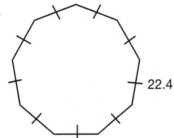

22.4

    b.

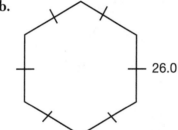

26.0

    c.

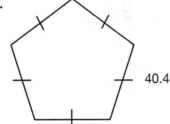

40.4

    d.

50.5

279. The measure of which figure's side is different from the other four figures?

a. a regular nonagon whose perimeter measures 90 feet

b. an equilateral triangle whose perimeter measures 27 feet

c. a regular heptagon whose perimeter measures 63 feet

d. a regular octagon whose perimeter measures 72 feet

e. It cannot be determined.

280. Which figure does not have 12 sides?

a. Regular Figure A with sides that measure 4.2 in. and a perimeter of 50.4 in.

b. Regular Figure B with sides that measure 1.1 in. and a perimeter of 13.2 in.

c. Regular Figure C with sides that measure 5.1 in. and a perimeter of 66.3 in.

d. Regular Figure D with sides that measure 6.0 in. and a perimeter of 72.0 in.

e. It cannot be determined.

Set 57

Find the perimeter of the following figures.

281.

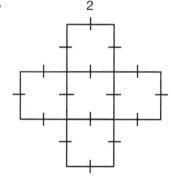

282.

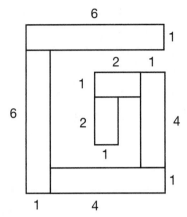

283.

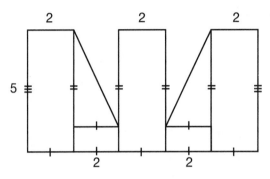

284.

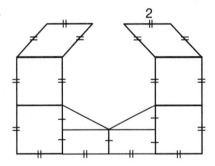

Set 58

Use the figure below to answer questions 285 through 286.

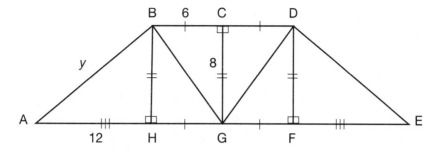

285. Find the value of *y*.

286. Find the figure's total perimeter.

Set 59

Use the figure below to answer questions 287 through 288.

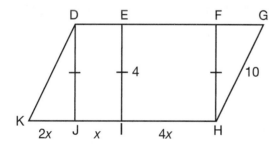

Given:
$\overline{DG} \cong \overline{KH}$
$\overline{KD} \cong \overline{HG}$

287. Find the value of *x*.

288. Find the figure's total perimeter.

Set 60

Use the figure below to answer questions 289 through 291.

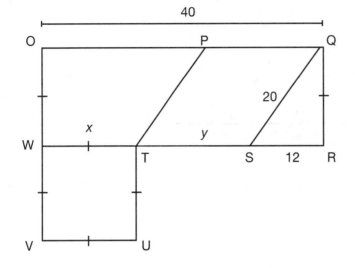

Given:
$\overline{OQ} \cong \overline{WR}$
$\overline{PQ} \cong \overline{TS}$

289. Find the value of x.

290. Find the value of y.

291. Find the figure's total perimeter.

Set 61

Use the figure below to answer questions 292 through 294.

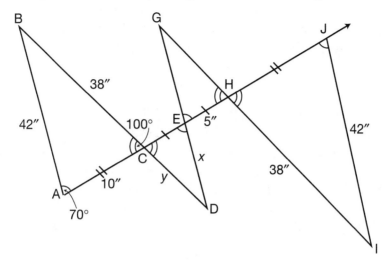

292. Find the value of x.

293. Find the value of y.

294. Find the figure's total perimeter.

Answers

Set 55

271. **a.** To find the perimeter, multiply the number of sides by the measure of one side. The perimeter of this Victorian gazebo is $p = 8 \times 5$.

272. **c.** Timmy walked ten ten-step sets. To find the perimeter of the figure Timmy walked, multiply 10 by 10 and remember that each side of that figure was measured in steps, not feet. Choice **a** forgot to count the first ten steps and turn that Timmy made. Choices **b** and **d** use the wrong increment, feet.

273. **c.** Plug the numbers into the formula: $p = ns$. $1600 = 4s$. $400 = s$.

274. **b.** A proportion can find an unknown side of a figure using known sides of a similar figure; a proportion can also find an unknown side using known perimeters. $\frac{93}{24} = \frac{31}{s}$. Cross-multiply: $93s = 31 (24)$.

275. **d.** Using a proportion find x. $\frac{12}{36} = \frac{4.5}{x}$. Cross-multiply. $12x = 36(4.5)$. $x = 13.5$. Polygon CRXZ is a rectangle whose sides measure 13.5, 54, 13.5, and 54. To find the perimeter of rectangle CRXZ, add the measures of its sides together.

Set 56

276. **b.** Each figure except trapezoid B has a perimeter of 84 feet; its perimeter measures only 80 feet.

277. **d.** Apply the formula $p = ns$ to each choice. In choice **a**, the perimeter of the backyard measures 12 feet × 4 sides, or 48 feet. In choice **b**, the perimeter of the pool measures 8 feet × 6 sides, or 48 feet. In choice **c**, the perimeter of the patio measures 6 feet × 8 sides, or 48 feet. In choice **d**, the perimeter of the Jacuzzi measures 4 feet by 10 sides, or 40. It is obvious that the Jacuzzi has a different perimeter.

278. **b.** Each figure has a perimeter of 202 feet except hexagon B; its perimeter measures 156 feet.

279. **a.** To find the measure of each side, change the formula $p = ns$ to $\frac{p}{n} = s$. Plug each choice into this formula. In choice **a**, the sides of the nonagon measure $\frac{90 \text{ feet}}{9 \text{ sides}}$, or 10 feet per side. In choice **b**, the sides of the triangle measure $\frac{27 \text{ feet}}{3 \text{ sides}}$, or 9 feet per side. In choice **c**, the sides of the heptagon measure $\frac{63 \text{ feet}}{7 \text{ sides}}$, or 9 feet per side. In choice d, the sides of the octagon measure $\frac{72 \text{ feet}}{8 \text{ sides}}$, or 9 feet per side.

280. **c.** To find the number of sides a figure has, change the formula $p = ns$ to $\frac{p}{s} = n$. Plug each choice into this formula. In choice **a**, figure A has 12 sides. In choice **b**, figure B has 12 sides. In choice **c**, figure C has 13 sides.

Set 57

281. $p = 24$. You can find this perimeter by either adding the measure of each side, or by using the formula $p = ns$. If you choose to add each side, your solution looks like this: $2 + 2 + 2 + 2 + 2 + 2 + 2 + 2 + 2 + 2 + 2 + 2 = 24$. If you choose to use the formula, there are five squares; four are exterior squares or $4p$ and one an interior square or $1p$. The final equation will look like $4p - 1p = P$. $1p = 4 \times 2$. $1p = 8$. $4p = 4 \times 8 = 32$. $32 - 8 = 24$.

282. $p = 50$. Using your knowledge of rectangles and their congruent sides, you find the measure of each exterior side not given. To find the perimeter, you add the measure of each exterior side together. $1 + 6 + 1 + 6 + 1 + 4 + 1 + 4 + 1 + 2 + 1 + 2 + 1 + 2 + 1 + 3 + 3 + 5 + 5 = 50$.

283. $p = 34 + 4\sqrt{5}$. First, find the hypotenuse of at least one of the two congruent triangles using the Pythagorean theorem: $2^2 + 4^2 = c^2$. $4^2 + 16^2 = c^2$. $20 = c^2$. $2\sqrt{5} = c$. Add the measure of each exterior side together: $2 + 5 + 2 + 2 + 2 + 2 + 2 + 5 + 2 + 2\sqrt{5} + 4 + 2 + 4 + 2\sqrt{5} = 34 + 4\sqrt{5}$.

284. $p = 32 + 2\sqrt{5}$. First find the hypotenuse of at least one of the two congruent triangles using the Pythagorean theorem: $1^2 + 2^2 = c^2$. $1 + 4 = c^2$. $\sqrt{5} = c$. Add the measure of each exterior side together. $2 + 2 + 2 + 2 + 2 + 2 + 2 + 2 + 2 + 2 + 2 + 2 + 2 + 2 + 2 + \sqrt{5} + \sqrt{5} = 32 + 2\sqrt{5}$.

Set 58

285. $y = 4\sqrt{13}$. $\overline{CG}$ and $\overline{BH}$ are congruent because the opposite sides of a rectangle are congruent. Plug the measurements of $\triangle ABH$ into the Pythagorean theorem: $12^2 + 8^2 = y^2$. $144 + 64 = y^2$. $208 = y^2$. $4\sqrt{13} = y$.

286. $p = 48 + 8\sqrt{13}$. Figure ABDE is an isosceles trapezoid; $\overline{AB}$ is congruent to $\overline{ED}$. Add the measure of each exterior line segment together: $6 + 6 + 4\sqrt{13} + 12 + 6 + 6 + 12 + 4\sqrt{13} = 48 + 8\sqrt{13}$.

Set 59

287. $x = \sqrt{21}$. In parallelogram DGHK, opposite sides are congruent, so $\triangle KDJ$ and $\triangle GFH$ are also congruent (Side-Side-Side postulate or Side-Angle-Side postulate). Plug the measurements of $\triangle KDJ$ and $\triangle GFH$ into the Pythagorean theorem: $(2x)^2 + 4^2 = 10^2$. $4x^2 + 16 = 100$. $4x^2 = 84$. $x^2 = 21$. $x = \sqrt{21}$.

288. $p = 14\sqrt{21} + 20$. Replace each x with $\sqrt{21}$ and add the exterior line segments together: $2\sqrt{21} + \sqrt{21} + 4\sqrt{21} + 10 + 2\sqrt{21} + 4\sqrt{21} + \sqrt{21} + 10 = 14\sqrt{21} + 20$.

Set 60

289. $x = 16$. The hatch marks indicate that $\overline{WT}$ and $\overline{QR}$ are congruent. Plug the measurements of $\triangle SQR$ into the Pythagorean theorem: $12^2 + x^2 = 20^2$. $144 + x^2 = 400$. $x^2 = 256$. $x = 16$.

290. $y = 12$. Opposite sides of a rectangle are congruent. $\overline{OQ}$ equals the sum of $\overline{WT}$, $\overline{TS}$, and $\overline{SR}$. Create the equation: $40 = 16 + y + 12$. $40 = 28 + y$. $12 = y$.

291. $p = 144$. Add the measure of each exterior line segment together:
$40 + 16 + 12 + 12 + 16 + 16 + 16 + 16 = 144$

Set 61

292. $x = 21$ **inches.** ΔABC and ΔJIH are congruent (Side-Side-Side postulate). ΔEDC and ΔEGH are also congruent because three angles and a side are congruent. However, ΔABC and ΔJIH are only similar to ΔEDC and ΔEGH (Angle-Angle postulate). A comparison of side $\overline{AC}$ to side $\overline{EC}$ reveals a 10:5 or 2:1 ratio between similar triangles. If $\overline{AB}$ measures 42 inches, then corresponding line segment $\overline{ED}$ measures half as much, or 21 inches.

293. $y = 19$. Using the same ratio determined above, if $\overline{BC}$ measures 38 inches, then corresponding line segment $\overline{DC}$ measures half as much, or 19 inches.

294. $p = 270$ **inches.** Add the measure of each exterior line segment together: $2(42 + 38 + 10) + 2(21 + 19 + 5) = 180 + 90 = 270$ inches.

13

Area of Polygons

Perimeter is the distance around an object. In this chapter you'll work with *area*, which is the amount of surface covered by an object. For example, the number of tiles on a kitchen floor would be found by using an area formula, while the amount of baseboard used to surround the room would be found by using a perimeter formula. Perimeter is always expressed in linear units. Area is always expressed in square units.

If the perimeter of a figure is the outline of a figure, then the **area** of a figure is what is inside the outline; area is the amount of two-dimensional space that a planar figure occupies.

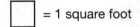
= 1 square foot

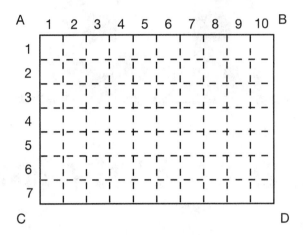

Polygon ABCD is 10 square feet by 7 square feet,
or 70 square feet

A square equals 1 foot by 1 foot
The area of polygon ABCD equals 10 squares by 7 squares,
or 70 square feet

The Area of a Parallelogram

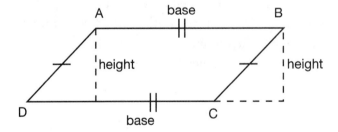

Area of parallelogram ABCD in square increments = base × height

The Area of a Rectangle

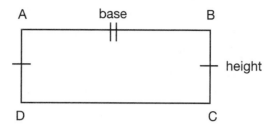

Area of rectangle ABCD in square increments = base × height

The Area of a Rhombus

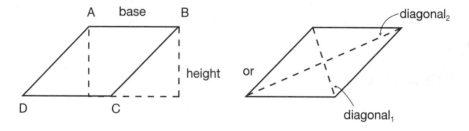

NOTE: a rhombus has
an area like a rectangle,
not a square

Area of rhombus ABCD in square increments = base × height
$\frac{1}{2}$(diagonal × diagonal)

The Area of a Square

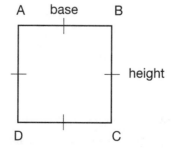

Area of square ABCD in square increments = base × height

The Area of a Triangle

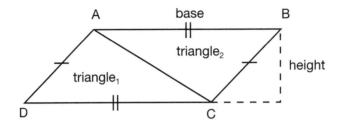

Triangle$_1$ ≅ triangle$_2$ therefore the area Δ_1 ≅ area Δ_2

Area $\Delta_1 = \frac{1}{2}$ Area of polygon ABCD

Area $\Delta_1 = \frac{1}{2}$ b · h

Area of ΔABC in square increments $= \frac{1}{2}$ base × height

The Area of a Trapezoid

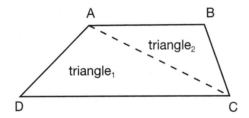

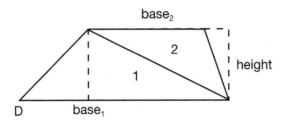

Area of Trapezoid ABCD = Area of Δ_1 + Area Δ_2

Area of Trapezoid ABCD $= \frac{1}{2}$ base$_1$ × height $+ \frac{1}{2}$ base$_2$ × height,

or $\frac{1}{2}$ height (base$_1$ + base$_2$)

Area of a trapezoid in square increments $= \frac{1}{2}$ height (base + base)

The Area of a Regular Polygon

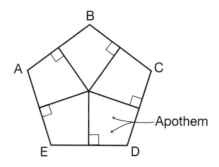

The area of regular polygon ABCDE in square increments
= apothem × perimeter

Similar Triangles

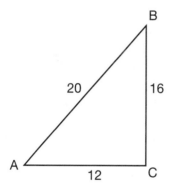

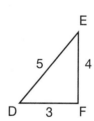

Triangle₁

Area $\Delta_1 = \frac{1}{2}(16)(12)$

96

Triangle₂

Area $\Delta_2 = \frac{1}{2}(4)(3)$

6

Ratio of Areas	Ratio of Corresponding Parts
$\Delta_1 : \Delta_2$	$\Delta_1 : \Delta_2$
96 : 6, or	$\overline{AB} : \overline{DE}$ 4 : 1 $\overline{BC} : \overline{EF}$ 4 : 1 $\overline{CA} : \overline{FD}$ 4 : 1
16 : 1	$(4 : 1)^2$

The ratio of areas between two similar triangles equals the square of the ratio of lengths between corresponding sides.

Set 62

Choose the best answer.

295. Area is
  a. the negative space inside a polygon.
  b. a positive number representing the interior space of a polygon.
  c. all the space on a plane.
  d. no space at all.

296. Two congruent figures have
  a. equal areas.
  b. disproportional perimeters.
  c. no congruent parts.
  d. dissimilar shapes.

297. The area of the figure below is the sum of which areas?

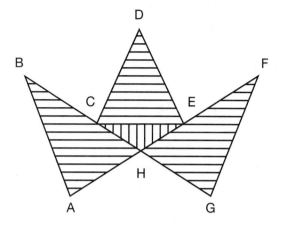

a. ΔABH + CDEH + ΔHFG + ΔCEH
b. ΔABH + ΔCDE + ΔHFG
c. ΔABH + ΔCDE + ΔHFG + ΔCEH
d. ΔABH + CDEH + ΔHFG + ΔAHG

298. If two triangles are similar, the ratio of their areas is
a. equal to the ratio of the lengths of any corresponding sides.
b. two times the ratio of the lengths of any corresponding sides.
c. equal to the square of the ratio of the lengths of any corresponding sides.
d. It cannot be determined.

299. An apothem
a. extends from the opposite side of a polygon.
b. bisects the side of a polygon to which it is drawn.
c. is drawn to a vertex of a polygon.
d. forms half of a central angle.

Set 63

Circle whether the statements below are true or false.

300. A rhombus with opposite sides that measure 5 feet has the same area as a square with opposite sides that measure 5 feet.
True or False.

301. A rectangle with opposite sides that measure 5 feet and 10 feet has the same area as a parallelogram with opposite sides that measure 5 feet and 10 feet. **True or False.**

302. A rectangle with opposite sides that measure 5 feet and 10 feet has twice the area of a square with opposite sides that measure 5 feet. **True or False.**

303. A parallelogram with opposite sides that measure 5 feet and 10 feet has twice the area of a rhombus with opposite sides that measure 5 feet. **True or False.**

304. A triangle with a base of 10 and a height of 5 has a third the area of a trapezoid with base lengths of 10 and 20 and a height of 5. **True or False.**

Set 64

Find the shaded area of each figure below.

305. Find the shaded area of ΔDEF.

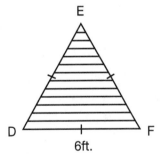

6ft.

306. Find the shaded area of quadrilateral ABCD.

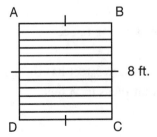

8 ft.

307. Find the shaded area of polygon KLMNO.

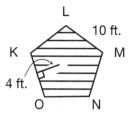

308. Find the shaded area of Figure X.

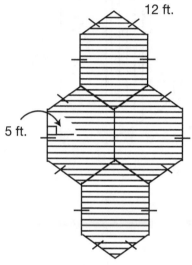

Figure X

309. Find the shaded area of Figure Y.

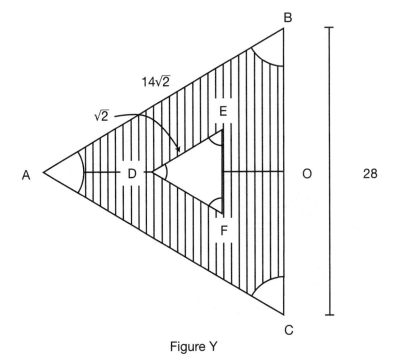

Figure Y

310. Find the shaded area of Figure Z.

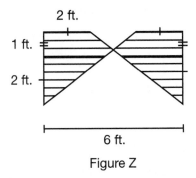

Figure Z

Set 65

Find the area of each figure below.

311. Find the area of quadrilateral ABCD.

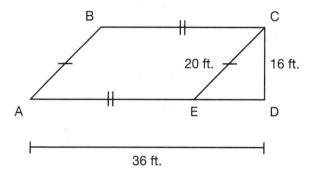

312. Find the area of polygon RSTUV.

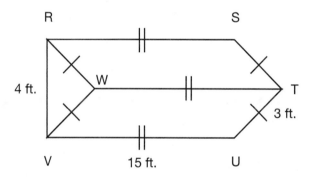

313. Find the area of concave polygon KLMNOPQR.

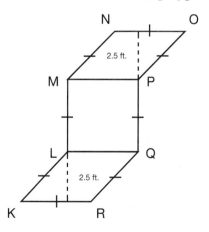

314. Find the area of polygon BCDEFGHI.

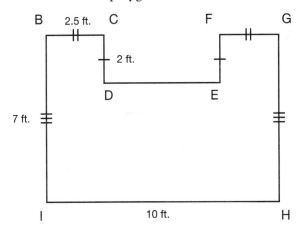

315. Find the area of concave polygon MNOPQR.

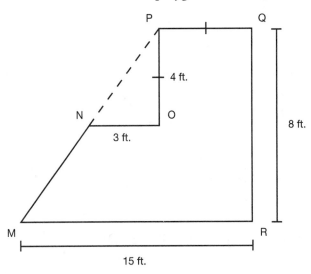

Set 66

Use the figure and information below to answer questions 316 through 319.

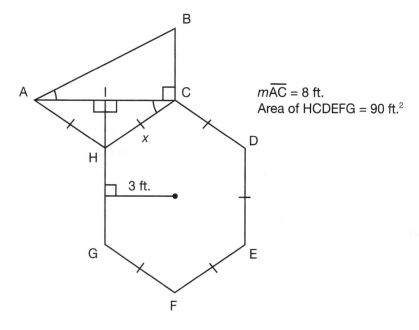

$m\overline{AC}$ = 8 ft.
Area of HCDEFG = 90 ft.^{2}

316. Find the length of $\overline{CH}$.

317. Find the area of $\triangle CHI$.

318. $\triangle CHI$ and $\triangle ABC$ are similar triangles. Find the area of $\triangle ABC$.

319. Find the entire area of figure ABCDEFGH.

Set 67

Use the figure and information below to answer questions 320 through 322.

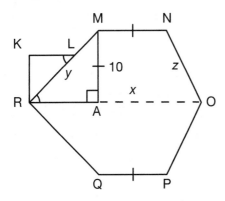

$\overline{RM} = y$

$\overline{NO} = z$

Area of RMNO = Area of RQPO

Area of RMNOPQ = 320 sq. ft.

Area of △RMA = 100 sq. ft.

320. Find the measure of side x.

321. Find the measure of side y.

322. Find the measure of side z.

Answers

Set 62

295. **b.** All areas are positive numbers. Choice **a** is incorrect because if an area represented negative space, then it would be a negative number, which it cannot be. Choice **c** is incorrect because the area of a plane is infinite; when you measure area, you are only measuring a part of that plane inside a polygon. Points, lines, and planes do not occupy space, but figures do. The area of a figure is how much space that figure occupies.

296. **a.** Congruent figures have congruent parts, perimeters, and areas.

297. **c.** The area of a closed figure is equal to the area of its **nonoverlapping** parts. This answer doesn't have to be broken down into all triangles—quadrilateral CDEH is a part of the figure. However, none of the answers can include quadrilateral CDEH and △CEH because they share interior points. Also, △AHG is not part of the closed figure; in fact, it isn't closed at all.

298. **c.** The ratio of areas between two similar triangles is equal to the square of the ratio of length of any two of their corresponding sides: Area of triangle: area of similar triangle = (length of side: length of corresponding side)^2.

299. **b.** An apothem extends from the center of a polygon to a side of the polygon. All apothems are perpendicular bisectors and only span half the length of a polygon. A radius (to be discussed in a later chapter) extends from the center point of a polygon to any vertex. Two consecutive radii form a central angle. Apothems are not radii.

Set 63

300. **False**. The area of the rhombus measures 20 square feet; while the area of the square measures 25 square feet. But isn't a rhombus a tilted square? Visually, a rhombus is a tilted square, but when you measure their areas, the height of a rhombus does not equal 5; it equals four. The rhombus has the area of a 5 by 4 foot rectangle.

301. **False**. The area of the parallelogram measures 40 square feet, while the area of the rectangle measures 50 square feet. The parallelogram has the area of a 4 by 10 rectangle.

302. **True**. If two squares can fit into one rectangle, then the rectangle has twice the area of one square.

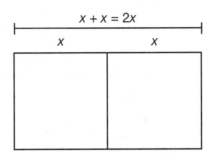

303. **True**. Like the squares and rectangle above, if two rhombuses can fit into one parallelogram, then the parallelogram has twice the area of one rhombus.

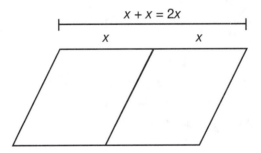

304. **True**. One triangle has an area of 25 square feet. The trapezoid has an area that measures 75 square feet. Three triangles fit into one trapezoid or the area of one triangle is a third of the area of the trapezoid.

Set 64

305. $18\sqrt{3}$ **square feet**. To find the height of equilateral $\triangle DEF$, draw a perpendicular line segment from vertex E to the midpoint of $\overline{DF}$. This line segment divides $\triangle DEF$ into two congruent right triangles. Plug the given measurement into the Pythagorean theorem: $(\frac{1}{2} \times 6)^2 + b^2 = 6^2$. $9 + b^2 = 36$. $b = \sqrt{27}$. $b = 3\sqrt{3}$.

To find the area, multiply the height by the base: $3\sqrt{3}$ feet $\times$ 6 feet $= 18\sqrt{3}$ square feet.

306. **64 square feet.** If one side of the square measures 8 feet, the other three sides of the square each measure 8 feet. Multiply two sides of the square to find the area: 8 feet $\times$ 8 feet = 64 square feet.

307. **100 square feet.** If one side of a regular pentagon measures 10 feet, the other sides of a pentagon measure 10 feet. If the perimeter of said pentagon measures 50 feet ($10 \times 5 = 50$) and its apothem measures 4 feet, then the area of the pentagon measures $\frac{1}{2} \times 4$ feet $\times$ 50 feet = 100 square feet.

308. **720 square feet.** The perimeter of a regular hexagon with sides 12 feet long equals 72 feet (12×6). When the apothem of said hexagon measures 5 feet, the area of the pentagon equals $\frac{1}{2} \times 5$ feet $\times$ 72 feet = 180 square feet. Since there are four conjoined regular hexagons, each with an area of 180 square feet, you multiply 180 square feet by 4. The honeycomb figure has a total area of 720 square feet.

309. **195 square feet.** The area of this shaded figure requires the dual use of the Pythagorean theorem and the ratio of areas between similar triangles. First, find half the area of $\triangle ABC$. Perpendicularly extend a line segment from vertex A to the midpoint of $\overline{CB}$. The height of right triangle ABO is 14^2 ft. $+ b^2 = (14\sqrt{2})^2$ ft. 196 sq. ft. $+ b^2 = 392$ sq. ft. $b^2 = 196$ sq. ft. $b = 14$ ft. Using the height, find the area of $\triangle ABC$: $\frac{1}{2}(14$ ft. $\times 28$ ft.$) = 196$ sq. ft. Within $\triangle ABC$ is a void, $\triangle DEF$. The area of the void must be subtracted from 196 square feet. If half that void is similar to $\triangle AOB$, then: $(\frac{14\sqrt{2}}{\sqrt{2}})^2 = \frac{98}{x}$. $\frac{392}{2} = \frac{98}{x}$. Cross-multiply: $392x = 196$, $x = \frac{1}{2}$ square feet. Half the void measures $\frac{1}{2}$ square feet; the total area of the void is 1 square foot. 196 sq. ft. $-$ 1 sq. ft. = 195 sq. ft.

310. **11 square feet.** Find the area of a rectangle with sides 6 feet and 3 feet: A = 6 ft. $\times$ 3 ft. A = 18 sq. ft. Find the area of both triangular voids: Area of the smaller triangular void = $\frac{1}{2}(2$ ft. $\times 1$ ft.$)$. Area = 1 sq. ft. Area of the larger triangular void = $\frac{1}{2}(6$ ft. $\times 2$ ft.$)$. Area = 6

sq. ft. Subtract 7 square feet from 18 square feet. 11 square feet remain.

Set 65

311. **480 square feet.** You can either treat figure ABCD like a trapezoid or like a parallelogram and a triangle. However you choose to work with the figure, you must begin by finding the measure of $\overline{ED}$ using the Pythagorean theorem: $16^2 + a^2 = 20$. $256 + a^2 = 400$. $a^2 = 144$. $a = 12$. Subtract 12 feet from 36 feet to find the measure of $\overline{BC}$: $36 - 12 = 24$. Should you choose to treat the figure like the sum of two polygons, to find the area of the entire figure, you find the area of each polygon separately and add them together. Parallelogram ABCE: 16 ft. × 24 ft. = 384 sq. ft. ΔECD: $\frac{1}{2}$ × 16 ft. × 12 ft. = 96 sq. ft. 384 sq. ft. + 96 sq. ft. = 480 sq. ft. Should you choose to treat the figure like a trapezoid and need to find the area, simply plug in the appropriate measurements: $\frac{1}{2}$ × 16 ft. (24 ft. + 36 ft.) = 480 square feet.

312. **$60 + 2\sqrt{5}$ square feet.** Extend $\overline{TW}$ to $\overline{RV}$. Let's call this $\overline{XW}$. $\overline{XW}$ perpendicularly bisects $\overline{RV}$; as a perpendicular bisector, it divides isosceles triangle RWV into two congruent right triangles and establishes the height for parallelograms RSTW and VUTW. Solve the area of parallelogram VUTW: 2 ft. × 15 ft. = 30 sq. ft. Find the height of ΔWXV using the Pythagorean theorem: $a^2 + 2^2 = 3^2$. $a^2 + 4 = 9$. $a^2 = 5$. $a = \sqrt{5}$. Solve the area of ΔZWV: $\frac{1}{2}$ × 5 ft. × 4 ft. = $2\sqrt{5}$ sq. ft. Add all the areas together: $2\sqrt{5}$ sq. ft. + 30 sq. ft. + 30 sq. ft. = $60 + 2\sqrt{5}$ square feet.

313. *Area* **= 24.0 square feet.** Rhombuses KLQR and MNOP are congruent. Their areas each equal 2.5 ft. × 3 ft. = 7.5 sq. ft. The area of square LMPQ equals the product of two sides: 3 ft. × 3 ft. = 9 ft. The sum of all the areas equal 9 sq. ft. + 7.5 sq. ft. + 7.5 sq. ft. = 24 square feet.

314. *Area* **= 60.0 square feet.** The simplest way to find the area of polygon BCDEFGHI is to find the area of rectangle BGHI: 10 ft. × 7 ft. = 70 sq. ft. Subtract the area of rectangle CFED: 5 ft. × 2 ft. = 10 sq. ft. 70 sq. ft. – 10 sq. ft. = 60 square feet.

315. *Area* **= 70 square feet.** Again, the simplest way to the find the area of polygon MNOPQR is to find the area of trapezoid MPQR. $\frac{1}{2} \times 8$ feet (4 ft. + 15 ft.) = $\frac{1}{2} \times 8(19)$ = 76 sq. ft. Subtract the area of ΔNPO: $\frac{1}{2} \times 3$ ft. × 4 ft. = 6 sq. ft. 76 sq. ft. – 6 sq ft. = 70 square feet.

Set 66

316. *x* **= 5 feet.** To find length *x*, you must use the given area of hexagon HCDEFG and work backwards. The area of a regular polygon equals the product of its perimeter by its apothem: 90 sq. ft. = $p \times 3$ ft. p = 30 ft. The perimeter of a regular polygon equals the length of each side multiplied by the number of sides: 30 ft. = s ft. × 6. s = 5 ft. $\overline{CH}$ equals one side of polygon HCDEFG; so, it is also 5 feet long.

317. *Area* **= 6 square feet.** ΔACH is an isosceles triangle. A line drawn from its vertex to $\overline{AC}$ bisects the line segment, which means $m\overline{AI}$ = $m\overline{CI}$, or $\frac{1}{2}$ of 8 feet long. Since question 316 found the measure of $\overline{HC}$, only the measure of $\overline{HI}$ remains unknown. Plug the given measurements for ΔCHI into the Pythagorean theorem. $4^2 + b^2$ = 5^2. $16 + b^2 = 25$. $b^2 = 9$. $b = 3$. Once the height is established, find the area of ΔCHI: $\frac{1}{2} \times 4$ ft. × 3 ft. = 6 square feet.

318. *Area* **= 24 square feet.** It is given that ΔCHI and ΔABC are similar triangles. You know the lengths of two corresponding sides, and you know the area of the smaller triangle. Apply the rule regarding the areas of similar triangles: $\frac{6 \text{ sq. ft.}}{x} = (\frac{4 \text{ ft.}}{8 \text{ ft.}})^2$. $\frac{6 \text{ sq. ft.}}{x}$ = $(\frac{1}{2})^2$. $\frac{6 \text{ sq. ft.}}{x} = \frac{1}{4}$. Cross-multiply: 6 sq. ft. × 4 = x. 24 square feet = x.

319. *Area* **= 126 square feet.** The areas within the entire figure are the sum of its parts: 24 sq. ft. + 6 sq. ft. + 6 sq. ft. + 90 sq. ft. = 126 square feet.

Set 67

320. *x* **= 22 feet.** The area of trapezoid RMNO plus the area of trapezoid RQPO equals the area of figure RMNOPQ. Since trapezoids RMNO and trapezoid RQPO are congruent, their areas are equal: $\frac{1}{2}$(320 sq. ft.) = 160 sq. ft. The congruent height of each trapezoid is known, and one congruent base length is known. Using the equation to find the area of a trapezoid, create the equation: 160 sq. ft. = $\frac{1}{2}$(10 ft.)(10 ft. + x). 160 sq. ft. = 50 sq. ft. + 5x ft. 110 sq. ft. = 5x ft. 22 feet = x.

321. **$y = 10\sqrt{2}$ feet.** Work backwards using the given area of ΔRMA: 50 sq. ft. = $\frac{1}{2}b$(10 ft.). 50 sq. ft. = 5 ft. × b. 10 ft. = b. Once the base and height of ΔRMA are established, use the Pythagorean theorem to find $\overline{RM}$: $10^2 + 10^2 = c^2$. $100 + 100 = c^2$. $200 = c^2$. $10\sqrt{2} = c$. $\overline{RM} = 10\sqrt{2}$ feet.

322. **$z = 2\sqrt{26}$ feet.** Imagine a perpendicular line from vertex N to the base of trapezoid RMNO. This imaginary line divides $\overline{RO}$ into another 10-foot segment. The remaining portion of line $\overline{RO}$ is 2 feet long. Use the Pythagorean theorem to find the length of $\overline{NO}$: 10 ft.^{2} + 2 ft.$^2 = z^2$. 100 sq. ft. + 4 sq. ft. = z^2. 104 sq. ft. = z^2. $2\sqrt{26}$ feet = z.

14

Surface Area of Prisms

A prism is the three-dimensional representation of planar figures, like rectangles or squares. To find the exterior area of a three-dimensional shape, called the **surface area**, simplify the prism or cube by breaking it down into its planar components.

Surface Area of a Prism

A prism has six faces; each face is a planar rectangle.

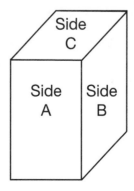

For every side or face you see, there is a congruent side you cannot see.

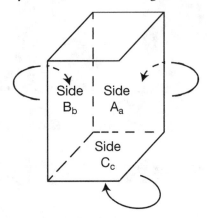

If you pull each face apart, you will see pairs of congruent rectangles.

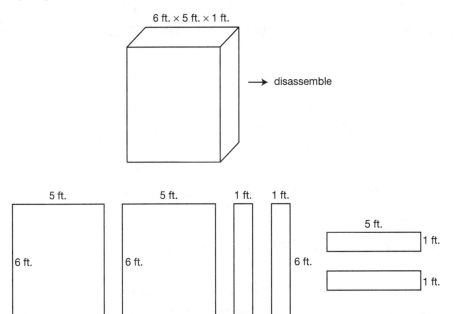

The surface area of a prism is the sum of the areas of its face areas, or *Sa* = (length × width) + (length × height) + (width × height) + (width × height) + (length × height) + (length × height). This formula simplifies into:

$$Sa = 2(lw + wh + lh)$$

Surface Area of a Cube

Like the rectangular prism, a cube has six faces; each face is a congruent square.

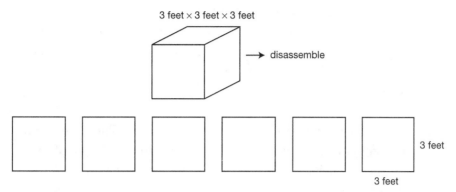

The surface area of a cube is the sum of its face areas, or Sa = (length × width) + (length × width) + (width × height) + (width × height) + (length × height) + (length × height). This formula simplifies into: $Sa = 6e^2$, where e is the measure of the edge of the cube, or length of one side.

Set 68

Choose the best answer.

323. A rectangular prism has
    a. one set of congruent sides.
    b. two pairs of congruent sides.
    c. three pairs of congruent sides.
    d. four pairs of congruent sides.

324. How many faces of a cube have equal areas?
    a. two
    b. three
    c. four
    d. six

Set 69

Find the surface area.

325. Mark plays a joke on Tom. He removes the bottom from a box of bookmarks. When Tom lifts the box, all the bookmarks fall out. What is the surface area of the empty box Tom is holding if the box measures 5.2 inches long by 17.6 inches high and 3.7 inches deep?

326. Crafty Tara decides to make each of her friends a light box. To let the light out, she removes a right triangle from each side of the box such that the area of each face of the box is the same. What is the remaining surface area of the box if each edge of the box measures 3.3 feet and the area of each triangle measures 6.2 square feet?

327. Jimmy gives his father the measurements of a table he wants built. If the drawing below represents that table, how much veneer does Jimmy's father need to buy in order to cover all the exterior surfaces of his son's table?

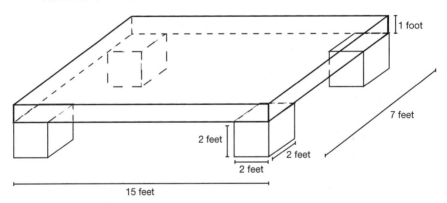

328. The 25th Annual Go–Cart Race is just around the corner, and Dave still needs to build a platform for the winner. In honor of the tradition's longevity, Dave wants the platform to be special; so, he will cover all the exposed surfaces of his platform in red velvet. If the base step measures 15 feet by 7 feet by 1 foot, and each consecutive step is uniformly 1 foot from the edge of the last step, how much exposed surface area must Dave cover?

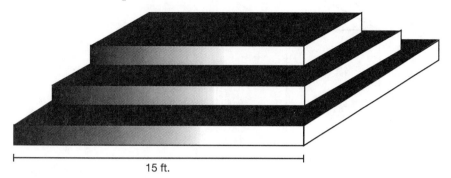

15 ft.

329. Sarah cuts three identical blocks of wood and joins them end-to-end. How much exposed surface area remains?

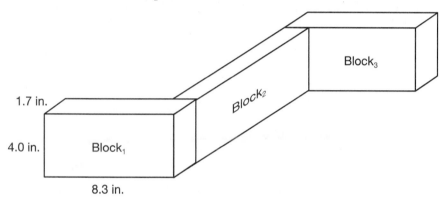

1.7 in.

4.0 in.   Block₁

8.3 in.

Sa Block₁ ≅ Sa Block₂ ≅ Sa Block₃

Set 70

Find each value of *x* using the figures and information below.

330. *Surface Area* = 304 square feet

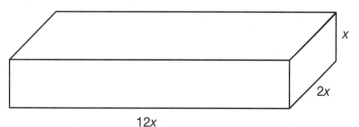

x

$2x$

$12x$

331. *Surface Area* = 990 square meters

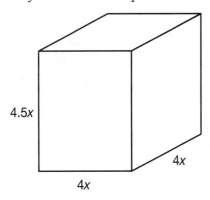

332. *Surface Area* = 862 square yards

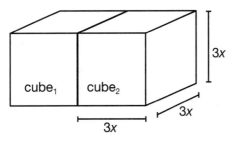

$cube_1 \cong cube_2$

Answers

Set 68

323. **c.** When the faces of a rectangular prism are laid side-by-side, you always have three pairs of congruent faces. That means every face of the prism (and there are six faces) has one other face that shares its shape, size, and area.

324. **d.** A cube, like a rectangular prism, has six faces. If you have a small box nearby, pick it up and count its faces. It has six. In fact, if it is a cube, it has six congruent faces.

Set 69

325. *Surface area* **= 260.24 square inches.** Begin by finding the whole surface area: surface area = $2(lw + wh + lh)$. $Sa = 2(17.6$ in.$(5.2$ in.$)$ + 5.2 in.$(3.7$ in.$)$ + 17.6 in.$(3.7$ in.$)$). $Sa = 2(91.52$ sq. in. + 19.24 sq. in. + 65.12 sq. in.$)$. $Sa = 2(175.88$ sq. in.$)$. $Sa = 351.76$ sq. in. From the total surface area, subtract the area of the missing face: Remaining $Sa = 351.76$ sq. in. $-$ 91.52 sq. in. Remaining $Sa =$ 260.24 square inches.

326. *Surface area* **= 28.14 square feet.** You could use the formula to determine the surface area of a rectangular prism to also determine the surface area of a cube, or you could simplify the equation to 6 times the square of the length of one side: $Sa = 6(3.3$ ft.$)^2$. $Sa =$ $6(10.89$ sq. ft.$)$. $Sa = 65.34$ sq. ft. Tara removes six triangular pieces, one from each face of the cube. It is given that each triangular cutout removes 6.2 sq. feet from the total surface area. 6 $\times$ 6.2 sq. ft. = 37.2 sq. ft. To find the remaining surface area, subtract the area removed from the surface area: 65.34 sq. ft. $-$ 37.2 sq. ft. = 28.14 square feet.

327. *Surface area* **= 318 square feet.** These next few problems are tricky: Carefully look at the diagram. Notice that the top of each cubed leg is not an exposed surface area, nor is the space they occupy under the large rectangular prism. Let's find these surface areas first. The top of each cubed leg equals the square of the length of the cube: (2 feet) = 4 sq. ft. There are four congruent cubes, four congruent faces: 4×4 sq. ft. = 16 sq. ft. It is reasonable to assume that where the cubes meet the rectangular prism, an equal amount of area from the prism is also not exposed. Total area concealed = 16 sq. ft + 16 sq. ft. = 32 sq. ft. Now find the total surface area of the table's individual parts.

Sa of one cube = $6(2 \text{ feet})^2 = 6(4 \text{ sq. ft.}) = 24$ sq. ft.

Sa of four congruent cubes = 4×24 sq. ft. = 96 sq. ft.

Sa of one rectangular prism = 2(15 ft.(7 ft.) + 7 ft.(1 foot) + 15 ft.(1 foot)) = 2(105 sq. ft. + 7 sq. ft. + 15 sq. ft.) = 2(127 sq. ft.) = 254 sq. ft.

Total *Sa* = 96 sq. ft. + 254 sq. ft. = 350 sq. ft.

Finally, subtract the concealed surface area from the total surface area = 350 sq. ft. – 32 sq. ft = 318 sq. ft.

328. *Surface area* **= 318 square feet.** Like the question above, there are concealed surface areas in this question. However, let's only solve exposed areas this time around. Find the surface area for the base rectangular prism. Do not worry about any concealed parts; imagine the top plane rising with each step. *Sa* of base rectangular prism = 2(15 ft.(7 ft.) + 7 ft.(1 foot) + 15 ft.(1 foot)) = 2(105 sq. ft. + 7 sq. ft. + 15 sq. ft.) = 2 (127 sq. ft.) = 254 sq. ft. Of the next two prisms, only their sides are considered exposed surfaces (the lip of their top surfaces have already been accounted for). The new formula removes the top and bottom planes: *Sa* of sides only = 2(*lh* + *wh*). Subtracting a foot from each side of the base prism, the second prism measures 13 feet by 5 feet by 1 foot. The last prism measures 11 feet by 3 feet by 1 foot. Plug the remaining two prisms into the formula:

Sa of sides only = 2(13 ft.(1 foot)) + 5 ft(1 foot)) = 2(13 sq. ft. + 5 sq. ft) = 2(18 sq. ft.) = 36 sq. ft.

Sa of sides only = 2(11 ft.(1 foot) + 3 ft.(1 foot)) = 2(11 sq. ft. + 3 sq. ft.) = 2(14 sq. ft.) = 28 sq. ft.

Add all the exposed surface areas together: 254 sq. ft. + 36 sq. ft. + 28 sq. ft = 318 sq. ft.

329. *Surface area* **= 297.5 sq. in.** The three blocks are congruent; find the surface area of one block and multiply it by three: *Sa* = 2(8.3 in.(4.0 in.) + 4.0 in. (1.7 in.) + 8.3 in.(1.7 in.) = 2(33.2 sq. in. + 6.8

sq. in. + 14.11 sq. in.) = 2(54.11 sq. in.) = 108.22 sq. in. 108.22 sq. in. × 3 = 324.66 sq. in. Look at the diagram: The ends of one block are concealed, and they conceal an equal amount of space on the other two blocks: 2 × 2(4.0 in.(1.7 in.) = 27.2 sq. in. Subtract the concealed surface area from the total surface area: 324.66 sq. in. − 27.2 sq. in. = 297.46 sq. in.

Set 70

330. $x = 2$ **feet.** Plug the variables into the formula for the Sa of a prism: 304 sq. ft. = $2(12x(2x) + 2x(x) + 12x(x))$. 304 sq. ft. = $2(24\,x^2 + 2x^2 + 12x^2)$. 304 sq. ft. = $2(38x^2)$. 304 sq. ft. = $76x^2$. 4 sq. ft. = x^2. 2 feet = x^2.

331. $x = 3$ **meters.** Plug the variables into the formula for the Sa of a prism: 990 square meters = $2(4.5x(4x) + 4x(4x) + 4.5x(4x))$. 990 sq. meters = $2(18x^2 + 16x^2 + 18x^2)$. 990 sq. meters = $2(52x^2)$. 990 sq. meters = $110x^2$. 9 sq. meters = x^2. 3 meters = x.

332. $x = 2\sqrt{2}$ **yards.** To find the area of one of the two congruent cubes, divide 864 square yards by 2: $\frac{864 \text{ sq. yd.}}{2}$ = 432 sq. yd. Plug the measure of each edge into the formula $Sa = 6\,e^2$: 432 sq. yd. = $6(3x^2)$. 432 sq. yd. = $6(9x^2)$. 432 sq. yd. = $54x^2$. 8 sq. yd. = x^2. $2\sqrt{2}$ yards = x.

15

Volume of Prisms and Pyramids

Is the cup half empty or half full? In geometry, it is neither half empty, nor half full; it is half the **volume**.

Volume is the space within a solid three-dimensional figure. Surface area defines the outer planes of a three-dimensional object; everything within is volume. Volume is what is inside the shapes you and I see.

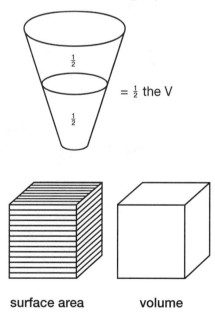

surface area   volume

Types of Prisms

You met rectangular and cubic prisms in the last chapter, and you exclusively used right prisms. The sides of a **right prism** perpendicularly meet the base. The base is the polygon that defines the shape of the solid.

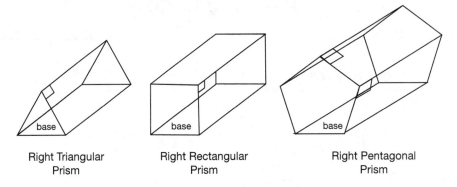

Right Triangular
Prism

Right Rectangular
Prism

Right Pentagonal
Prism

The sides of an **oblique prism** do not meet the base at a 90° angle. Again, that base can be any polygon.

The most common oblique prism is the **Pyramid**.

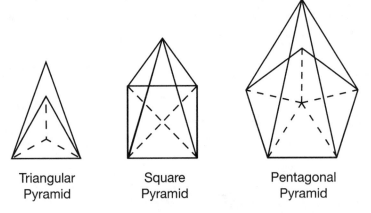

Triangular
Pyramid

Square
Pyramid

Pentagonal
Pyramid

The Volume of a Right Prism

The volume of a right prism = area of its base × height

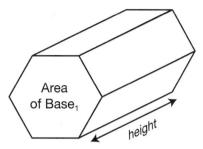

The volume of a right rectangular prism = area of its base × height, or
length × width × height

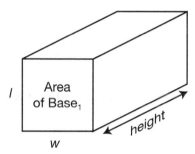

The volume of a right cube = area of its base × height, or
length × width × height, or
(the measure of one edge)

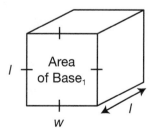

The Volume of a Pyramid

The volume of a pyramid = $\frac{1}{3}$ (area of its base × height)
It is a third of the volume of a right prism with the same base and height measurements.

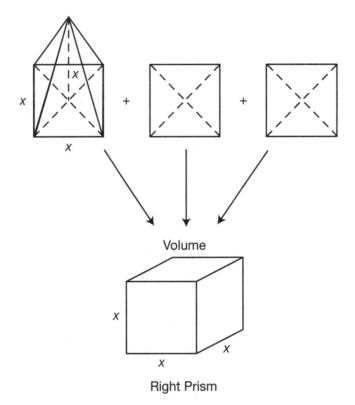

Volume

Right Prism

Set 71

Choose the best answer.

333. Which figure below is a right prism?

a.

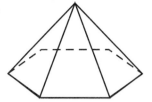

b.

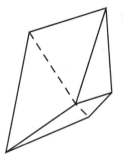

c.

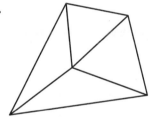

d.

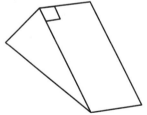

334. Which polygon defines the shape of the right prism below?

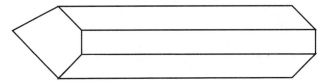

    a. triangle
    b. rectangle
    c. square
    d. pentagon

335. What is the name of a right 12-sided prism?
    a. an octagonal prism
    b. decagonal prism
    c. dodecagon
    d. tetradecagon

336. Which figure below is a right hexagonal prism?

a.

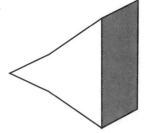

b.

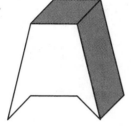

c.

d.

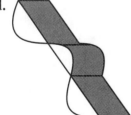

337. Which choice describes a figure that has a third of the volume of the figure below?

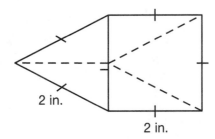

2 in.

2 in.

    a. a right triangular prism with base sides that measure 2 in. and a height that measures 2 in.

    b. a cube with base sides that measure 2 in. and a height that measures 2 in.

    c. a triangular pyramid with base sides that measure 2 in. and a height that measures 2 in.

    d. a square pyramid with base sides that measure 2 in. and a height that measures 2 in.

338. Which figure below has a third of the volume of a 3 in. cube?

a. 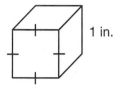 1 in.

b. 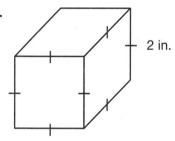 2 in.

c. 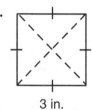 3 in.

d. 1 in.

339. Which measurement uses the largest increment?
   a. perimeter
   b. area
   c. surface area
   d. volume

Set 72

Find the volume of each solid.

340. Find the volume of a right heptagonal prism with base sides that measure 13 cm, an apothem that measures 6 cm, and a height that measures 2 cm.

341. Find the volume of a pyramid with four congruent base sides. The length of each base side and the prism's height measure 2.4 ft.

342. Find the volume of a pyramid with an eight-sided base that measures 330 sq. in. and a height that measures 10 in.

Set 73

Find each unknown element using the information below.

343. Find the height of a right rectangular prism with a 295.2 cubic in. volume and a base area that measures 72.0 sq. in.

344. Find the base area of a right nonagon prism with an 8,800 cubic ft. volume and a height that measures 8.8 ft.

345. Find the measure of a triangular pyramid's base side if its volume measures $72\sqrt{3}$ cubic meters and its height measures 6 meters. The base of the pyramid forms an equilateral triangle.

Set 74

Use the solid figure below to answer questions 346 through 348.

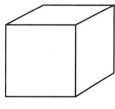

l = 2.1 meters

346. What is the perimeter of one face side?

347. What is the surface area?

348. What is the volume?

Set 75

Use the solid figure below to answer questions 349 through 351.

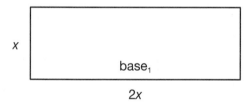

perimeter of base = 54 in.
volume = 810 in.[3]

349. What is the width and length?

350. What is the height?

351. What is the surface area?

Answers

Set 71

333. **d.** Choice **a** is a hexagonal pyramid; none of its six sides perpendicularly meets its base. The sides of choice **b** only perpendicularly join one base side, and choice **c** is an oblique quadrilateral; its base is facing away from you. Choice **d** is the correct answer; it is a triangular right prism.

334. **d.** The solid in the figure has seven sides. Subtract two base sides, and it has five sides, one for each edge of a pentagon. You will be tempted to answer *rectangle*. Remember all right prisms have rectangles. It is the polygon at the base of the rectangle that defines the prism's shape.

335. **b.** Do as you did above: subtract two base sides—the prism has ten sides, one for each edge of a decagon.

336. **b.** A hexagonal prism must have a hexagon as one of its sides. A right hexagonal prism has two hexagons. Choice **a** is a pentagonal right prism; choice **c** is a decagonal right prism; and choice **d** is not a prism at all.

337. **c.** If their base measurements are congruent, a pyramid's volume is a third of a prism's volume. Choices **a** and **b** are eliminated because they are not pyramids. Choice **d** is also eliminated because its base polygon is not equivalent to the given base polygon, an equilateral triangle.

338. **c.** Again, you are looking for a pyramid with the same base measurements of the given cube. Twenty-seven choice **a**'s can fit into the given cube; meanwhile, eighty-one choice **d**'s fit into that same cube. Only three choice **c**'s fit into the given cube; it has one-third the volume.

339. **d.** Perimeter uses a single measurement like an inch to describe the outline of a figure. Area and Surface area use square measurements, an inch times an inch, to describe two-dimensional space. Volume uses the largest measurement; it uses the cubic measurement, an inch times an inch times an inch. Volume is three-dimensional; its measurement must account for each dimension.

Set 72

340. *Volume* **= 1,092 cubic centimeters.** The area of a seven-sided figure equals the sum of the measures of its sides multiplied by its apothem: *perimeter of heptagonal base* = 13 sides × 7 cm = 91 cm. *Area of heptagonal base* = 91 cm × 6 cm = 546 square cm. The volume of a right prism with heptagonal bases is the area of one base multiplied by the prism's height: *volume of prism* = 546 square cm × 2 cm = 1,092 cubic cm.

341. *Volume* **= 4.6 cubic feet.** This is a square based pyramid; its volume is a third of a cube's volume with the same base measurements, or $\frac{1}{3} bh$. Plug its measurements into the formula: $\frac{1}{3}$(2.4 ft.) × 2.4 ft. *Volume of square pyramid* = $\frac{1}{3}$(5.76 sq. ft.) × 2.4 ft. = $\frac{1}{3}$(13.824 cubic ft.) = 4.608 cubic ft.

342. *Volume* **= 1,100 cubic inches.** Unlike the example above, this pyramid has an octagonal base. However, it is still a third of a right octagonal prism with the same base measurements, or $\frac{1}{3} bh$. Conveniently, the area of the base has been given to you: *area of octagonal base* = 330 square inches. *Volume of octagonal pyramid* = $\frac{1}{3}$(330 sq. in) × 10 in. = $\frac{1}{3}$(3,300 cubic in.) = 1,100 cubic in.

Set 73

343. *Height* **= 4.1 inches.** If the volume of a right rectangular prism measures 295.2 cubic inches, and the area of one of its two congruent bases measures 72.0 square inches, then its height measures 4.1 inches: 295.2 cubic in. = 72.0 square in. × h. 4.1 in. = h.

344. *Area* **= 1,000 square feet.** If the volume of a right nonagon prism measures 8,800 cubic feet and its height is 8.8 feet, then the area of one of its two congruent bases measures 1,000 square feet: 8,800 cubic ft. = $B \times 8.8$ feet. 1,000 square ft = B.

345. *Side* **= 12 meters.** If the volume of a triangular pyramid is $72\sqrt{3}$ cubic meters, work backwards to find the area of its triangular base and then the length of a side of that base (remember, you are working with regular polygons, so the base will be an equilateral triangle). $72\sqrt{3}$ cubic meters = $\frac{1}{3}$ *area of base* $\times$ 6 meters. $72\sqrt{3}$ cubic meters = $a \times 2$ meters. $36\sqrt{3}$ square meters = a. Divide both sides by $6\sqrt{3}$ meters. $36\sqrt{3}$ square meters = $\frac{1}{2}$ side of base $\times 6\sqrt{3}$ meters. 6 meters = $\frac{1}{2}b$. 12 meters = b.

Set 74

346. *Perimeter* **= 8.4 meters.** A cube has six congruent faces; each face has four congruent sides. The perimeter of a single cube face is the sum of the measure of each edge, or $p = 4s$. $p = 4(2.1$ meters). $p = 8.4$ meters.

347. *Surface area* **= 26.5 square meters.** The surface area of a cube is the area of one face multiplied by the number of faces, or $Sa = 6bh$. $Sa = 6(2.1$ meters). $Sa = 6(4.41$ square meters). $Sa = 26.46$ square meters.

348. *Volume* **= 9.3 cubic meters.** The volume of a cube is its length multiplied by its width multiplied by its height, or $V = e^2$ (e represents one edge of a cube). $V = 2.1$ meters $\times 2.1$ meters $\times 2.1$ meters. $V = 9.261$ cubic meters.

Set 75

349. *Length* **= 18 inches;** *width* **= 9 inches.** Plug the given variables and perimeter into the formula $p = l + w + l + w$. 54 in. = $2x + x + 2x + x$. 54 in. = $6x$. 9 inches = x.

350. *Height* **= 5 inches.** Multiply the length and width above: 18 inches $\times$ 9 inches = 162 square inches. This is the area of one base side. Using the given volume and the area above, find the third side of rectangular prism A: 810 cubic in. = 162 sq. in. $\times h$. 5 inches = h.

351. *Surface area* **= 594 square inches.** The surface area of a prism is a sum of areas, or $Sa = 2(lw + wh + lh)$. Plug the measures you found in the previous question into this formula. $Sa = 2(18 \text{ in.} \times 9 \text{ in.}) + (9 \text{ in.} \times 5 \text{ in.}) + (18 \text{ in.} \times 5 \text{ in.})$. $Sa = 2(162 \text{ sq. in.} + 45 \text{ sq. in.} + 90 \text{ sq. in.})$. $Sa = 2 (297 \text{ sq. in.})$. $Sa = 594$ square inches.

16

Working with Circles and Circular Figures

Part A

It is said that circles have no beginnings and no ends; and yet as you start this chapter, you have just come full circle. To properly review circles, we start with a point.

Center Point, Radius, Central Angle

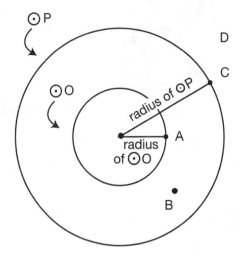

Points in relationship to Circle P

- B is an interior point to ⊙P

- C is on ⊙P

- D is an exterior to ⊙P

A **center point** is a stationary point at the "center" of a circle. All the points that lie on the circle are equidistant from the center point.

A **radius** is a line segment that extends from the center of the circle and meets exactly one point on the circle.

Circles with the same center point but different radii are **concentric circles**.

A **central angle** is an angle formed by two radii.

Chords and Diameters

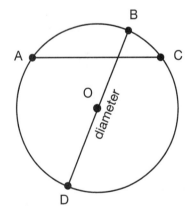

$\overline{OB}$ and $\overline{OD}$ are each a radius of ⊙O.

$\overline{DB}$ is a diameter
$\overline{AC}$ is a chord

$\overline{OB} \cong \overline{OD}$
$2 \times m\overline{OB} = m\overline{DB}$

A **chord** is a line segment that joins two points on a circle.

A **diameter** is a chord that joins two points on a circle and passes through the center point.

Note: A diameter is twice the length of a radius, and a radius is half the length of a diameter.

Arcs

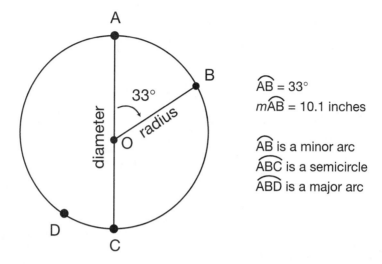

$\overset{\frown}{AB} = 33°$

$m\overset{\frown}{AB} = 10.1$ inches

$\overset{\frown}{AB}$ is a minor arc
$\overset{\frown}{ABC}$ is a semicircle
$\overset{\frown}{ABD}$ is a major arc

An **arc** is a set of consecutive points on a circle. Arcs can be measured by their rotation and by their length.

A **minor arc** is an arc that measures less than 180°.

A **semicircle** is an arc that measures exactly 180°. The endpoints of a semicircle are the endpoints of a diameter.

A **major arc** is an arc that measures greater than 180°.

Note: An arc formed by a central angle has the same rotation of that angle.

Other Lines and Circles

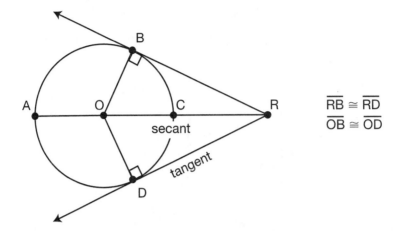

$$\overline{RB} \cong \overline{RD}$$
$$\overline{OB} \cong \overline{OD}$$

A **tangent** is a ray or line segment that intercepts a circle at exactly one point. The angle formed by a radius and a tangent where it meets a circle is a right angle.

Note: Two tangents from the same exterior point are congruent.

A **secant** is a ray or line segment that intercepts a circle at two points.

Congruent Arcs and Circles

Congruent circles have congruent radii and diameters. Congruent central angles form congruent arcs in congruent circles.

Set 76

Choose the best answer.

352. Which points of a circle are on the same plane?
   a. only the center point and points on the circle
   b. points on the circle but no interior points
   c. the center point, interior points, but no points on the circle
   d. all the points in and on a circle

353. In a circle, a radius
    a. is the same length of a radius in a congruent circle.
    b. extends outside the circle.
    c. is twice the length of a diameter.
    d. determines an arc.

354. Congruent circles
    a. have the same center point.
    b. have diameters of the same length.
    c. have radii of the same length.
    d. **b** and **c**

Use the figure below to answer question 355.

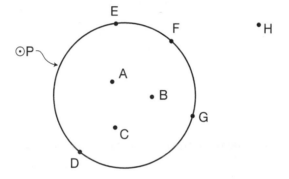

355. Which point(s) is an exterior point?
    a. A, B, C
    b. D, E, F, G
    c. H
    d. A, E, G, H

356. •A lies 12 inches from the center of ⊙P. If ⊙P has a 1-foot radius.
    •A lies
    a. inside the circle.
    b. on the circle.
    c. outside the circle.
    d. between concentric circles.

357. A diameter is also
   a. a radius.
   b. an arc.
   c. a chord.
   d. a line.

358. Both tangents and radii
   a. extend from the center of a circle.
   b. are half a circle's length.
   c. meet a circle at exactly one point.
   d. are straight angles.

359. From a stationary point, Billy throws four balls in four directions. Where each ball lands determines the radius of another circle. What do the four circles have in common?
   a. a center point
   b. a radius
   c. a diameter
   d. a tangent

360. From a stationary point, Kim aims two arrows at a bull's-eye. The first arrow nicks one point on the edge of the bull's-eye; the other strikes the center of the bull's-eye. Kim knows the first arrow traveled 100 miles. If the bull's-eye is 200 miles wide, how far is Kim from the center of the bull's-eye?
   a. 100 miles
   b. $2\sqrt{100}$ miles
   c. 1,000 miles
   d. $100\sqrt{2}$ miles

Set 77

Use the figure below to answer question 361.

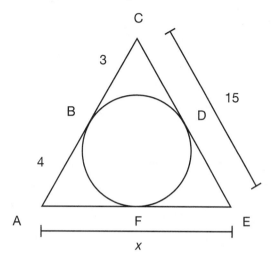

361. What is the value of x?

Use the figure below to answer question 362.

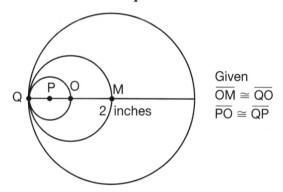

362. If the diameter of ⊙M is 2 inches, then what is the diameter of ⊙P?

Use the figure below to answer question 363.

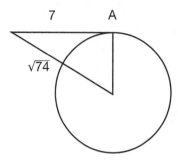

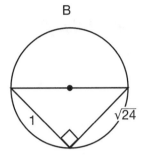

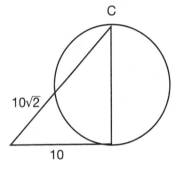

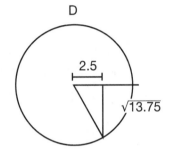

363. Which circle is NOT congruent?

Use the figures below to answer question 364.

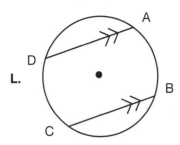

L.

$\overset{\frown}{AB} \cong \overset{\frown}{CD}$

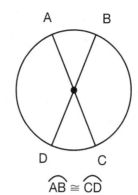

P.

$\overset{\frown}{AB} \cong \overset{\frown}{CD}$

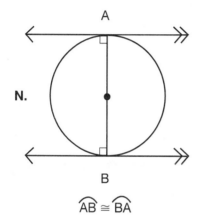

N.

$\overset{\frown}{AB} \cong \overset{\frown}{BA}$

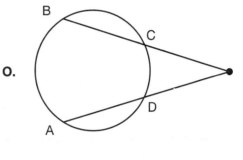

O.

$\overset{\frown}{AB} \cong \overset{\frown}{CD}$

364. In which figure (L, N, P, O) is the set of arcs not congruent?

Use the figure below to answer questions 365 through 367.

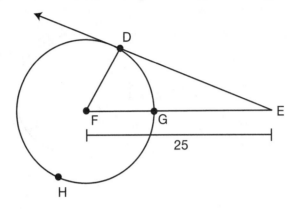

365. What is the length of a radius in the circle?

366. What is the area of ΔDEF?

367. Is $\overparen{DHG}$ a major or minor arc?

Part B

When you measure the edge of a circle, where and when do you stop if there isn't a vertex? You could go in circles trying to figure it out. Fortunately, you don't have to. Greek mathematicians measured it for you and called it *pi*. Actually, they named it the Greek letter *pi*, whose symbol looks like a miniature Stonehenge (π). The value of π is *approximately* (≈) $\frac{22}{7}$, or 3.14.

The Circumference of a Circle

The circumference of a circle is the circle's version of perimeter. *Circa* means *around*. Sailors circumnavigate the earth; they navigate their way around the earth.

Circumference of a circle = π × diameter, or
π × 2 times the radius

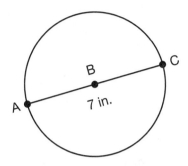

$2 \times m\overline{AB} = m\overline{AC}$
$C = \pi 2r$
$C = \pi 2 \times 7$ inches
$C = \pi 14$ inches

The Measure of an Arc

Using the circumference of a circle, you can find the measure of an arc.

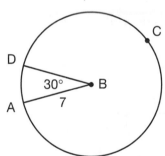

$C = \pi 14$ inches
$$\frac{30°}{360°} = \frac{1}{12}$$
$\overarc{AD}$ is $\frac{1}{12}$ of π14 inches, or
$\pi\frac{7}{16}$ inches

Area of a Circle

Area of a circle in square units = π × radius²

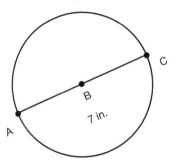

$A = \pi r^2$

$A = \pi(7 \text{ inches})^2$

$A = 49\pi \text{ square inches}$

Set 78

Choose the best answer.

368. What is the perimeter of the figure below?

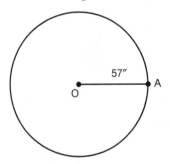

a. 57π inches
b. 114π inches
c. 26.5π inches
d. $\sqrt{57\pi}$ inches

369. What is the area of the figure below?

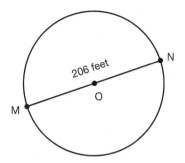

  a. 51.5π square feet
  b. 103π square feet
  c. 206π square feet
  d. $10,609\pi$ square feet

370. What is the radius of the figure below?

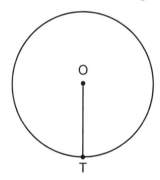

perimeter of ⊙O= 64π centimeters

  a. 8 centimeters
  b. 16 centimeters
  c. 32 centimeters
  d. 64 centimeters

371. The area of a square is 484 square feet. What is the maximum area of a circle inscribed in the square?
  a. 11π square feet
  b. 22π square feet
  c. 121π square feet
  d. 122π square feet

372. If the circumference of a circle is 192π feet, then the length of the circle's radius is
   a. $16\sqrt{6}$ feet.
   b. 96 feet.
   c. 192 feet.
   d. 384 feet.

373. If the area of a circle is 289π square feet, then the length of the circle's radius is
   a. 17 feet.
   b. 34 feet.
   c. 144.5 feet.
   d. 289 feet.

374. What is the area of a circle inscribed in a dodecagon with an apothem 13 meters long?
   a. 26π meters
   b. 156π meters
   c. 42.2π meters
   d. 169π meters

Use the figure below to answer questions 375 through 376.

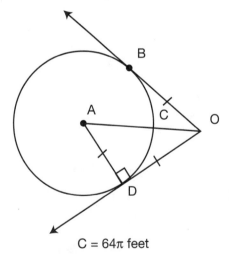

C = 64π feet

375. $\overset{\frown}{BD}$ is a quarter of the circumference of $\odot C$. If the total circumference of $\odot C$ is 64π feet, then what is the length of $\overset{\frown}{BD}$?
a. 16π feet
b. 32π feet
c. 48π feet
d. 90π feet

376. What is the central angle that intercepts $\overset{\frown}{BD}$?
a. an acute angle
b. a right angle
c. an obtuse angle
d. a straight angle

Use the figure below to answer question 377.

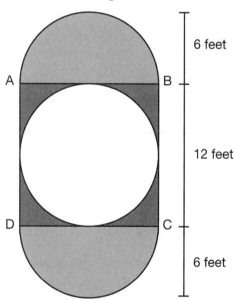

377. What is the area of the shaded figure?
a. 144 square feet – 12π square feet
b. 12 square feet – 144π square feet
c. 144 square feet
d. 144 square feet – 24π square feet + 12π square feet

Set 79

Use the figure below to answer questions 378 through 379.

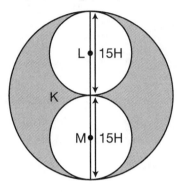

378. What is the area of the shaded figure?
- **a.** 56.25π square feet
- **b.** 112.4π square feet
- **c.** 225π square feet
- **d.** 337.4π square feet

379. What is the ratio of the area of ⊙K and the area of ⊙M?
- **a.** 1:8
- **b.** 1:4
- **c.** 1:2
- **d.** 1:1

Use the figure below to answer questions 380 through 381.

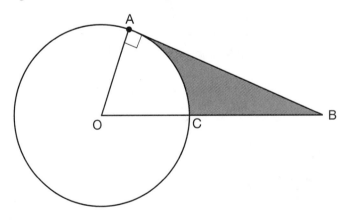

380. If $m\overline{AB} = 60$ and $m\overline{OB} = 75$, what is the measure of $\overline{OA}$?

381. If central angle AOC measures 60°, what is the area of the shaded figure?

Use the figure below to answer questions 382 through 383.

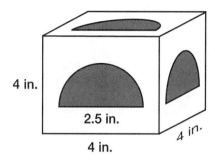

4 in.

2.5 in.

4 in.

4 in.

382. If each side of a cube has an identical semicircle carved into it, what is the total carved area of the cube?

383. What is the remaining surface area of the cube?

Using the figure below answer questions 384 through 387.

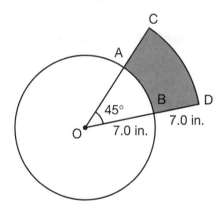

384. Find the shaded area of the figure.

385. Find the measure of $\overset{\frown}{AB}$.

386. Find the measure of $\overset{\frown}{CD}$.

387. Are $\overset{\frown}{AB}$ and $\overset{\frown}{CD}$ congruent?

Set 80

Use the figure below to answer questions 388 through 389.

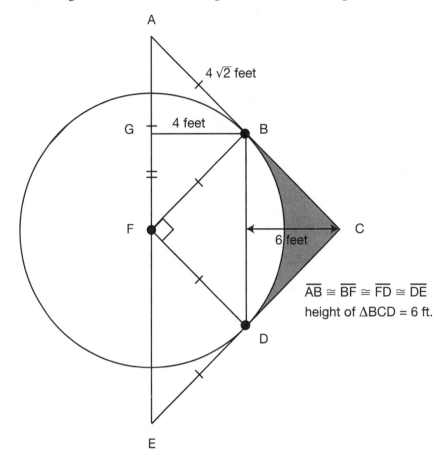

388. What is the area of trapezoid ABDE?

389. What is the shaded area?

Part C

When a balloon deflates or a basketball goes flat, the spherical object loses a part of its volume made of air. Unlike a prism, a sphere does not have a set of straight sides that you can measure. Its volume and surface area must be deduced.

The Surface Area of a Cylinder (A Right Prism with Circular Bases)

Surface Area of a cylinder in squared units $=$ the sum of the area of its sides, or $2\pi r^2 + 2\pi rh$

The Volume of a Cylinder

Volume of a cylinder in cubic units = area of its base × height, or $\pi(r^2)h$

The Volume of a Cone

Volume of a cone in cubic units $= \frac{1}{3}$ the area of its base × height, or $\frac{1}{3}\pi(r^2)h$

The Surface Area of a Sphere

A sphere is a set of points equidistant from one central point. Imagine a circle; rotate that circle in every direction around a stationary center point. You have created the shape of a sphere and witnessed that no matter what slice of the sphere you take, if it is cut through the center point, it is a circle.

Surface area of a sphere in square units $= 4\pi r^2$

The Volume of a Sphere

Volume of a sphere in cubic units $= \frac{4}{3}\pi r^3$

Set 81

Use the figure below to answer questions 390 through 392.

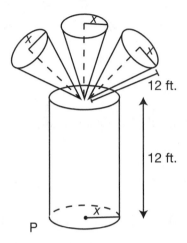

Volume of cylinder P = 432π cubic ft.

390. If the volume of the cylinder P is 432π cubic feet, what is the length of x?

391. What is the surface area of cylinder P?

392. What is the total volume of the solid?

Set 82

Use the figure below to answer questions 393 through 395.

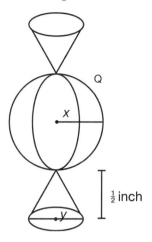

Volume Q = $\frac{1}{6}\pi$ cubic inches

393. If the volume of a candy wrapper Q is $\frac{1}{6}\pi$ cubic inches, what is the length of x?

394. If the conical ends of candy wrapper Q have $\frac{1}{96}\pi$ cubic inch volumes each, what is the length of y?

395. What is the surface area of the candy inside the wrapper?

Set 83

Solve each question using the information in each word problem.

396. Tracy and Jarret try to share an ice cream cone, but Tracy wants half of the scoop of ice cream on top while Jarret wants the ice cream inside the cone. Assuming the half scoop of ice cream on top is a perfect sphere, who will have more ice cream? The cone and scoop both have radii 1 inch long; the cone is 3 inches high.

397. Dillon fills the cylindrical coffee grind containers each day. One bag has 32π cubic inches of grinds. How many cylindrical containers can Dillon fill with two bags of grinds if each cylinder is 4 inches wide and 4 inches high?

398. Before dinner, Jen measures the circumference and length of her roast. It measures 12π round and 4 inches long. After cooking, the roast is half its volume but just as long. What is the new circumference of the roast?

399. Mike owns many compact discs (CDs), that he has to organize. If his CD holder is 5 inches wide by 3 inches high by 10 inches long and his CDs measure 4 inches wide by an eighth of an inch long, how many CDs fit back-to-back in Mike's CD case?

400. Munine is trying to carry her new 24-inch tall cylindrical speakers through her front door. Unfortunately, they do not fit upright through the width of the doorway. If each speaker is $2,400\pi$ cubic inches, what is the maximum width of her doorway assuming $pi \approx 3.14$.

401. Tory knows that the space in a local cathedral dome is $13,122\pi$ cubic feet. Using her knowledge of geometry, what does Tory calculate the height of the dome to be?

Set 84

402. In art class, Billy adheres 32 identical half spheres to canvas. What is their total surface area, not including the flat side adhered to the canvas, if the radius of one sphere is 8 centimeters?

403. Joe carves a perfect 3.0-meter wide sphere inside a right prism. If the volume of the prism is 250.0 cubic meters, how much material did he remove? How much material remains?

404. Theoretically, how many spherical shaped candies should fit into a cylindrical jar if the diameter of each candy is 0.50 inch, and the jar is 4.50 inches wide and 6 inches long?

405. A sphere with a 2-foot radius rests inside a cube with edges 4.5 feet long. What is the volume of the space between the sphere and the cube assuming $pi \approx 3.14$?

Set 85

Use Puppet Dan to answer questions 406 through 414.

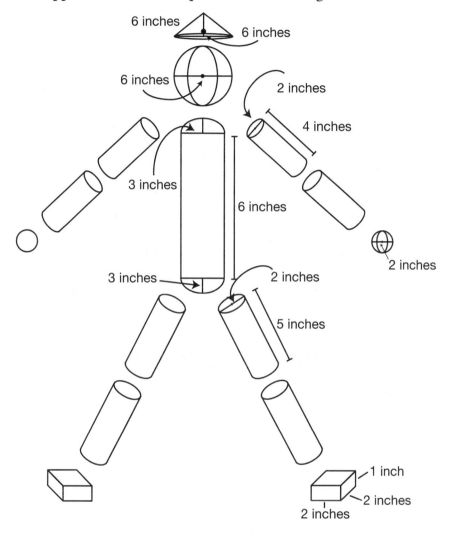

6 inches   6 inches

6 inches

2 inches

4 inches

3 inches

6 inches

2 inches

3 inches

2 inches

5 inches

1 inch

2 inches

2 inches

406. What is the volume of Puppet Dan's hat if it measures 6 inches wide by 6 inches high?

407. What is the volume of Puppet Dan's head if it measures 6 inches wide?

408. What is the volume of Puppet Dan's arms if one segment measures 2 inches wide by 4 inches long?

409. What is the volume of Puppet Dan's hands if each one measures 2 inches wide?

410. What is the volume of Puppet Dan's body if it measures 3 inches wide and 6 inches long? Each end of the cylinder measures 6 inches wide.

411. What is the volume of Puppet Dan's legs if each segment measures 2 inches wide by 5 inches long?

412. What is the volume of Puppet Dan's feet if each foot measures 2 inches × 2 inches × 1 inch?

413. What is puppet Dan's total volume?

414. Puppet Dan is made out of foam. If foam weighs 3 ounces per cubic inch, how much does the total of puppet Dan's parts weigh?

Answers

Set 76

352. **d.** All the points of a circle are on the same plane; that includes the points on a circle (points on the circumference), the center point, interior points, and exterior points (unless otherwise stated).

353. **a.** A circle is a set of points equidistant from a center point. Congruent circles have points that lie the same distance from two different center points. Consequently, the radii (the line segments that connect the center point to the points on a circle) of congruent circles are congruent. Choices **b** and **c** are incorrect because they describe secants. Choice **d** describes a chord.

354. **d.** Congruent circles have congruent radii; if their radii are congruent, then their diameters are also congruent. Choice **a** describes concentric circles, not congruent circles.

355. **c.** An exterior point is a point that lies outside a circle. Choice **a** represents a set of interior points. Choice **b** represents a set of points on ⊙P; and choice **d** is a mix of points in, on, and outside of ⊙P.

356. **b.** 12 inches is a foot, so •A lies on ⊙P. If the distance from •A to the center point measured less than the radius, then •A would rest inside ⊙P. If the distance from •A to the center point measured greater than the radius, then •A would rest outside of ⊙P.

357. **c.** A diameter is a special chord; it is a line segment that bridges a circle *and passes through the center point.*

358. **c.** As a tangent skims by a circle, it intercepts a point on that circle. A radius spans the distance between the center point of a circle and a point on the circle; like a tangent, a radius meets exactly one point on a circle.

359. **a.** Billy acts as the central fixed point of each of these four circles, and circles with a common center point are concentric.

360. **d.** A bull's-eye is a circle; the flight path of each arrow is a line. The first arrow is a tangent that also forms the leg of a right triangle. The path of the second arrow forms the hypotenuse. Use the Pythagorean theorem to find the distance between Kim and the center of the bull's-eye: 100 miles^2 + 100 miles^2 = c^2. 10,000 sq. miles + 10,000 sq. miles = c^2. 20,000 sq. miles = c^2. $100\sqrt{2} = c$.

Set 77

361. $x = 16$. Tangent lines drawn from a single exterior point are congruent to each of their points of interception with the circle; therefore, x is the sum of lengths $\overline{AF}$ and $\overline{EF}$ where $\overline{AF}$ is congruent to $\overline{AB}$, and $\overline{EF}$ is congruent to $\overline{ED}$. $\overline{AB}$ is 4, and $\overline{DE}$ is the difference of $\overline{CE}$ and $\overline{CD}$, or 12; x is 4 plus 12, or 16.

362. **Diameter ⊙P = 0.25.** ⊙O is half of ⊙M; its diameter measures 0.50. ⊙P is half of ⊙O; its diameter measures 0.25.

363. **⊙B.** Use the Pythagorean theorem to find the length of each circle's radius:

⊙A: $7^2 + b^2 = \sqrt{74}^2$. $49 + b^2 = 74$. $b^2 = 25$. $b = 5$. *Radius* = 5.

⊙B: $1^2 + \sqrt{24}^2 = c^2$. $1 + 24 = c^2$. $25 = c^2$. $5 = c$. *Radius* = $\frac{1}{2}(5) = 2.5$.

⊙C: $10^2 + b^2 = 10\sqrt{2}^2$. $100 + b^2 = 200$. $b^2 = 100$. $b = 10$. *Radius* = $\frac{1}{2}(10) = 5$.

⊙D: $2.5^2 + \sqrt{13.75}^2 = c^2$. $6.25 + 13.75 = c^2$. $25 = c^2$. $5 = c$. *Radius* = 5.

Only ⊙B is not congruent to ⊙A, ⊙C, and ⊙D.

364. **⊙O.** Parallel lines form congruent arcs. Two diameters form congruent arcs. Parallel tangent lines form congruent semi-circles. Secants extending from a fixed exterior point form non-congruent arcs.

365. *Radius* = 15. Draw an imaginary radius between the center point and the point of interception between the tangent and the circle. The radius (G) and the tangent form a right angle. Use the

Pythagorean theorem to find the length of $\overline{DF}$: $a^2 + 20^2 = 25^2$. $a^2 + 400 = 625$. $a^2 = 225$. $a = 15$.

366. ***Area* = 150 square inches.** The length of $\overline{ED}$ is the height of $\triangle DEF$. To find the area of $\triangle DEF$, plug the measures of the radius and the height into $\frac{1}{2}bh$: $\frac{1}{2}$(15 in. × 20 in.) = 150 square inches.

367. $\overset{\frown}{DHG}$ is a major arc.

Set 78

368. **b.** The perimeter of a circle is twice the radius times *pi*: (2 × 57 inches)π.

369. **d.** The area of a circle is the radius squared times *pi*: (103 feet²)π.

370. **c.** If the perimeter of a circle is 64π centimeters, then the radius of that circle is half of 64, or 32 centimeters.

371. **d.** If the area of a square is 484 square feet, then the sides of the square must measure 22 feet each. The diameter of an inscribed circle has the same length as one side of the square. The maximum area of an inscribed circle is π(11 feet²), or 121π square feet.

372. **b.** The circumference of a circle is *pi* times twice the radius. 192 feet is twice the length of the radius; therefore half of 192 feet, or 96 feet, is the actual length of the radius.

373. **a.** The area of a circle is *pi* times the square of its radius. If 289 feet is the square of the circle's radius, then 17 feet is the length of its radius. Choice **c** is not the answer because 144.5 is half of 289, not the square root of 289.

374. **d.** If the apothem of a dodecagon is 13 meters, then the radii of an inscribed circle are also 13 meters. The area of the circle is π(13 meters²), or 169π square meters.

375. **a.** The length of arc BD is a quarter of the circumference of ⊙C, or 16π feet.

376. **b.** A quarter of 360° is 90°; it is a right angle.

377. **c.** This question is much simpler than it seems. The half circles that cap square ABCD form the same area as the circular void in the center. Find the area of square ABCD, and that is your answer. 12 feet × 12 feet = 144 feet. Choice **a** and **d** are the same answer. Choice **b** is a negative area and is incorrect.

Set 79

378. **b.** The radii of ⊙L and ⊙M are half the radius of ⊙K. Their areas equal π(7.5 feet²), or 56.3π square feet each. The area of ⊙K is π(15²), or 225π square feet. Subtract the areas of circles L and M from the area of ⊙K: 225π sq. ft. – 112.6π sq. ft. = 112.4π square feet.

379. **b.** Though ⊙M has half the radius of ⊙K, it has a fourth of the area of ⊙K. 56.25π square feet: 225.0π square feet, or 1:4.

380. **Radius = 45 feet.** Use the Pythagorean theorem: $a^2 + 60^2 = 75^2$. $a^2 + 3,600 = 5,625$. $a^2 = 2,025$. $a = 45$ feet.

381. **The area of ⊙O is π(45 feet²),** or 2,025π square feet. If central angle AOC measures 60°, then the area inside the central angle is $\frac{1}{6}$ the total area of ⊙O, or 337.5π square feet. The area of ΔABO is $\frac{1}{2}$(45 feet × 60 feet), or 540 square feet. Subtract the area inside the central angle from the area of the triangle: shaded area = 540 square feet – 337.5π square feet.

382. **The area of one semicircle is** $\frac{1}{2}\pi(r^2)$: A = $\frac{1}{2}\pi(2.5$ in.²). A ≈ 3.1π square inches. Multiply the area of one semicircle by 6: **6 × 3.1π square inches ≈ 18.6π square inches.**

383. The surface area of a cube is 6(4 inches²), or 96 square inches. Subtract the area of six semicircles from the surface area of the cube: **remaining surface area = 96 square inches – 18.6π square inches.**

384. *Area* **= 18.4π square inches.** $\overparen{CD}$ is part of a concentric circle outside ⊙O. Its area is π(14 inches)^2, or 196π square inches. A 45° slice of that area is one-eighth the total area, or 24.5π square inches. This is still not the answer. The area of ⊙O is π(7 inches)^2, or 49π square inches. Again, a 45° slice of that area is one-eighth the total area, or 6.1π square inches. Subtract the smaller wedge from the larger wedge, and the shaded area is 18.4π square inches.

385. **1.8π inches.** The circumference of ⊙O is 14π inches. A 45° slice of that circumference is one-eighth the circumference, or 1.8π inches.

386. **3.5π inches.** The circumference of concentric ⊙O is 28π inches. An eighth of that circumference is 3.5π inches.

387. **No.** $\overparen{AB}$ and $\overparen{CD}$ may have the same rotation, but they do not have the same length.

Set 80

388. *Area* **= 48 square feet.** Use the Pythagorean theorem to find $\overline{AG}$. $4\sqrt{2}$ ft.^{2} = 4 ft.^{2} + b^2. 32 sq. ft. = 16 sq. ft. + b^2. b = 4 ft. If $\overline{AG}$ equals 4 feet, then $\overline{AF}$ and $\overline{EF}$ equal 8 feet, and $\overline{AE}$ equals 16 feet. The area of a trapezoid is half its height times the sum of its bases: $\frac{1}{2}$(4 ft.)(8 ft. + 16 ft.) = 2(24) = 48 square feet.

389. *Area* **≈ 14.88 square feet.** The shaded area is the difference of ΔBCD's area and the area between chord BD and arc BD. The height of ΔBCD is 6 feet. Its area is $\frac{1}{2}$(6 ft. × 8 ft.) = 24 sq. ft. The area of $\overparen{BD}$ is tricky. It is the area of the circle contained within ∠BFD minus the area of inscribed ΔBFD. Central angle BFD is a right angle; it is a quarter of a circle's rotation and a quarter of its area. The circle's radius is $4\sqrt{2}$ feet. The area of circle F is π(4$\sqrt{2}$ ft.)^2, or 32π square feet. A quarter of that area is 8π square feet. The area of ΔBFD is $\frac{1}{2}$(4 ft. × 8 ft.) = 16 sq. ft. Subtract 16 square feet from 8π square feet, then subtract that answer from 24 square feet and your answer is approximately 14.88 square feet.

Set 81

390. $x = 6$ **feet.** The radius of cylinder P is represented by x; it is the only missing variable in the volume formula. Plug in and solve: 432π cubic ft. $= (\pi x^2)12$ ft. 36 sq. ft. $= x^2$. 6 feet $= x$.

391. *Surface area* $= 216\pi$ **square feet.** The surface area of a cylinder is $2\pi r^2 + 2\pi rh$: Plug the variables in and solve: $Sa = 2\pi(6$ ft$)^2 + 2\pi(6$ ft. $\times 12$ ft.$)$. 72π sq. ft.$+ 144\pi$ sq. ft. $= 216\pi$ sq. ft.

392. *Total volume* $= 864\pi$ **cubic feet.** This problem is easier than you think. Each cone has exactly the same volume. The three cones together equal the volume of the cylinder. Multiply the volume of the cylinder by 2, and you have the combined volume of all three cones and the cylinder.

Set 82

393. $x = \frac{1}{2}$ **inch.** The volume of a sphere is $\frac{4}{3}\pi r^3$, where x is the value of r. Plug the variables in and solve: $\frac{1}{6}\pi$ cubic in. $= \frac{4}{3}\pi x^3$. $\frac{1}{8}$ cubic in. $= x^3$. $\frac{1}{2}$ inch $= x$.

394. $y = \frac{1}{4}$ **inch.** The volume of a cone is $\frac{1}{3}\pi r^2 h$, where y is the value of r. Plug in the variables and solve: $\frac{1}{96}\pi$ cubic in. $= \frac{1}{3}\pi y^2 2\frac{1}{2}$ in. $\frac{1}{96}\pi$ cubic in. $= \frac{1}{6}\pi y^2$. $\frac{1}{16}\pi$ sq. in. $= y^2$. $\frac{1}{4}$ inch $= y$.

395. *Surface area* $= 1.0\pi$ **square inch.** The candy inside the wrapper is a perfect sphere. Its surface area is $4\pi r^2$. Plug the variables in and solve: $Sa = 4\pi(0.5$ inch $^2)$. $Sa = 1.0\pi$ square inch.

Set 83

396. **Jarret.** The volume of a half sphere is $\frac{1}{2}(\frac{4}{3}\pi r^3)$. Tracy's half scoop is then $\frac{1}{2}(\frac{4}{3}\pi \times 1$ inch$^3)$, or $\frac{2}{3}\pi$ cubic inches. The volume of a cone is $\frac{1}{3}\pi r^2 h$. The ice cream in the cone is $\frac{1}{3}\pi(1$ inch$^2 \times 3$ inches$)$, or π cubic inches. Jarret has $\frac{1}{3}\pi$ cubic inches more ice cream than Tracy.

397. **4 containers.** The volume of each container is $\pi(2 \text{ inches}^2 \times 4$ inches), or 16π cubic inches. One bag fills the volume of two containers. Two bags will fill the volume of four containers.

398. **Circumference = $6\sqrt{2}\pi$ inches.** This is a multi step problem. Find the radius of the roast: $2\pi r = 12\pi$ inches. $r = 6$ inches. The volume of the roast is $\pi(6 \text{ inches}^2 \times 4 \text{ inches})$, or 144π cubic inches. After cooking, the roast is half is original volume, or 72π cubic inches. Its new radius is 72π cubic inches $= \pi r^2 \times 4$ inches. $r = 3\sqrt{2}$ inches. The new circumference of the roast is $2\pi r$, or $6\sqrt{2}\pi$ inches.

399. **80 discs.** This problem is not as hard as it might seem. A 4-inch-wide disc's diameter is 4 inches. Its circumference is 4π inches; it will fit snugly in a box with a 15-square-inch face. To find how many CDs will sit back-to-back in this container, divide the length of the container by the thickness of each disc: $\frac{10 \text{ inches}}{0.125 \text{ inches per disc}} =$ 80 discs.

400. **Less than 20 inches.** The radius of a single speaker is $\pi(r^2 \times 24$ inches) $= 2,400\pi$ cubic inches. $r^2 = 100$ square inches. $r = 10$ inches. The width of each speaker is twice the radius, or 20 inches. Munine's door is less than 20 inches wide!

401. **27 feet.** Half the volume of a sphere is $\frac{1}{2}(\frac{4}{3}\pi r^3)$, or $\frac{2}{3}\pi r^3$. If the volume is $13,122\pi$ cubic feet, then the radius is 27 feet. The height of the dome is equal to the radius of the dome; therefore the height is also 27 feet.

Set 84

402. **4,096π square centimeters.** Surface area of a whole sphere is $4\pi r^2$. The surface area of half a sphere is $2\pi r^2$. Each sphere's surface area is $2\pi(8 \text{ centimeters}^2)$, or 128π square centimeters. Now, multiply the surface area of one half sphere by 32 because there are 32 halves: $32 \times 128\pi$ square centimeters $= 4,096\pi$ square centimeters.

403. **Approximately 235.9 cubic meters.** Joe removed the same amount of material as volume in the sphere, or $\frac{4}{3}\pi(1.5 \text{ meters}^3)$, which simplifies to 4.5π cubic meters. The remaining volume is 250 cubic meters – 4.5π cubic meters, or approximately 235.9 cubic meters.

404. **1,518 candies.** The volume of each candy is $\frac{4}{3}\pi(0.25 \text{ inches}^3)$, or 0.02π cubic inches. The volume of the jar is $\pi(2.25 \text{ inches}^2 \times 6)$ inches, or 30.36π cubic inches. Divide the volume of the jar by the volume of a candy ($\frac{30.36\pi \text{ cubic inches}}{0.02\pi \text{ cubic inches}}$), and 1,518 candies can theoretically fit into the given jar (not including the space between candies).

405. *Remaining volume* ≈ **57.6 ft.** First, find the volume of the cube, which is 4.5 feet^3, or approximately 91.1 cubic feet. The volume of the sphere within is only $\frac{4}{3}\pi(2 \text{ feet}^3)$, or approximately 33.5 cubic feet. Subtract the volume of the sphere from the volume of the cube. The remaining volume is approximately 57.6 cubic feet.

Set 85

406. Volume of a cone = $\frac{1}{3}\pi r^2 h$. $V = \frac{1}{3}\pi(3 \text{ in.}^2 \times 6 \text{ in.})$. ***V* = 18π cubic inches.**

407. Volume of a sphere = $\frac{4}{3}\pi r^3$. $V = \frac{4}{3}\pi(3 \text{ in.}^3)$. ***V* = 36π cubic inches.**

408. Volume of a cylinder = $\pi r^2 h$. $V = \pi(1 \text{ in.}^2 \times 4 \text{ in.})$ $V = 4\pi$ cubic inches. There are four arm segments, so four times the volume = **16π cubic inches.**

409. Volume of a sphere = $\frac{4}{3}\pi r^3$. $V = \frac{4}{3}\pi(1 \text{ in.}^3)$. $V = \frac{4}{3}\pi$ cubic inches. There are two handballs, so two times the volume = $\frac{8}{3}\pi$ **cubic inches.**

410. The body is the sum of two congruent half spheres, which is really one sphere, and a cylinder. *Volume of a sphere* = $\frac{4}{3}\pi r^3$. $V = \frac{4}{3}\pi 3$ in.^{3}. $V = 36\pi$ cubic inches. *Volume of a cylinder* = $\pi r^2 h$. $V = \pi(3$ in.$^2 \times 6$ in.$)$ $V = 54\pi$ cubic inches. *Total volume* = **90π cubic inches.**

411. Volume of a cylinder = $\pi r^2 h$. $V = \pi(1$ in.$^2 \times 5$ in.$)$ $V = 5\pi$ cubic inches. There are four leg segments, so four times the volume = **20π cubic inches.**

412. Each foot is a rectangular prism. *Volume of a prism* = *length* × *width* × *height*. $V = 2$ in. × 2 in. × 1 in. $V = 4$ cubic inches. There are two feet, so two times the volume = **8 cubic inches.**

413. The sum of the volumes of its parts equals a total volume. 18π cubic inches + 36π cubic inches + 16π cubic inches + $\frac{8}{3}\pi$ cubic inches + 90π cubic inches + 20π cubic inches ≈ 182.6π cubic inches + 8 cubic inches. If π ≈ 3.14, then V ≈ **581.36 cubic inches.**

414. Multiply: $\frac{3 \text{ ounces}}{1 \text{ cubic inch}}$ × 581.36 cubic inches = **1,744.08 ounces.** Puppet Dan is surprisingly light for all his volume!

17

Coordinate Geometry

Geometry is about the relationships of objects in space. A point is a location in space; a line is a series of locations in space; a plane is an expanse of locations in space. Seem familiar? It all should; it is Chapter 1 revisited. But if space is infinitely long and wide, how do you locate something that doesn't take up space? To locate points in space, graph a grid by drawing horizontal and vertical lines.

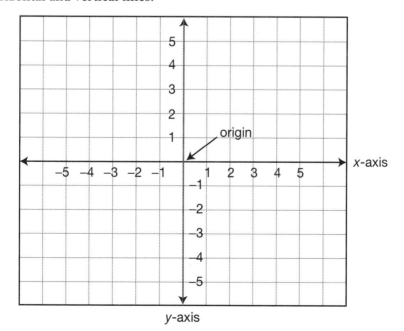

A point's position left or right of the origin is its *x*-coordinate; a point's position up or down from the *x*-axis is its *y*-coordinate. Every point has a coordinate pair: (spaces left or right of the *y*-axis, spaces above or below the *x*-axis).

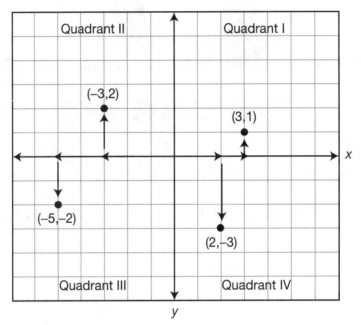

Plotting a Point on a Coordinate Plane

To plot a point from the origin, look at the coordinate pair. Using the first coordinate, count the number of spaces indicated right (*x* > 0) or left (*x* < 0) of the origin. Using the second coordinate, count the number of spaces indicated up (*y* > 0) or down (*y* < 0) of the *x*-axis.

The Length of a Line

On a grid, every diagonal line segment has length and height; it is the hypotenuse of an imaginary right triangle. Its length is the square root of the sum of the square length of each leg. (It is the Pythagorean theorem revisited.)

$$a = x - x$$

$$b = y - y$$

$c = d$ (the distance between two points)

$c^2 = a^2 + b^2$ (Pythagorean Theorem)

$$d^2 = (x - x)^2 + (y - y)^2$$

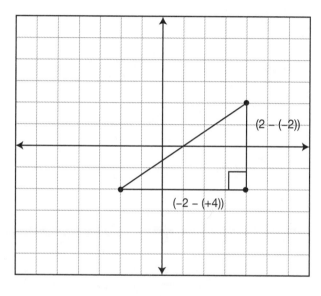

$(2 - (-2))$

$(-2 - (+4))$

Pythagorean theorem
$a^2 + b^2 + c^2$
$\sqrt{a^2 + b^2} = c$

Distance $= \sqrt{\Delta x^2 + \Delta y^2}$
$D = \sqrt{(-2 - 4)^2 + (2 - -2)^2}$
$D = \sqrt{(-6)^2 + (4)^2}$
$D = \sqrt{36 + 16}$

Set 86

Choose the best answer.

415. The origin is
  a. where the x-axis begins.
  b. where the y-axis begins.
  c. where the x-axis intersects the y-axis.
  d. not a location.

416. •A (–3,–2) lies in quadrant
   a. I.
   b. II.
   c. III.
   d. IV.

417. •M (–109,.3) lies in quadrant
   a. I.
   b. II.
   c. III.
   d. IV.

418. •Q (.01,100) lies in quadrant
   a. I.
   b. II.
   c. III.
   d. IV.

419. •R is 3 spaces right and one space above •P (–1,–2). •R lies in
   quadrant
   a. I.
   b. II.
   c. III.
   d. IV.

420. •B is 40 spaces left and .02 spaces above •A (20,.18). •B lies in
   quadrant
   a. I.
   b. II.
   c. III.
   d. IV.

421. •O is 15 spaces right and 15 spaces below •N (–15,0). •O lies on
   a. x-axis.
   b. y-axis.
   c. z-axis.
   d. the origin.

422. On a coordinate plane, $y = 0$ is
    a. the x-axis.
    b. the y-axis.
    c. a solid line.
    d. finitely long.

423. A baseball field is divided into quadrants. The pitcher is the point of origin. The second baseman and the hitter lie on the y-axis; the first baseman and the third baseman lie on the x-axis. If the hitter bats a ball into the far left field, the ball lies in quadrant
    a. I.
    b. II.
    c. III.
    d. IV.

424. •A $(12,3)$, •B $(0,3)$ and •C $(-12,3)$ are
    a. noncoplanar.
    b. collinear.
    c. noncollinear.
    d. a line.

425. •G $(14,-2)$, •H $(-1,15)$ and •I $(3,0)$
    a. determine a plane.
    b. are collinear.
    c. are noncoplanar.
    d. are a line.

426. The distance between •J $(4,-5)$ and •K $(-2,0)$ is
    a. $\sqrt{11}$.
    b. $\sqrt{29}$.
    c. $\sqrt{61}$.
    d. $\sqrt{22}$.

Set 87

State the coordinate pair for each point.

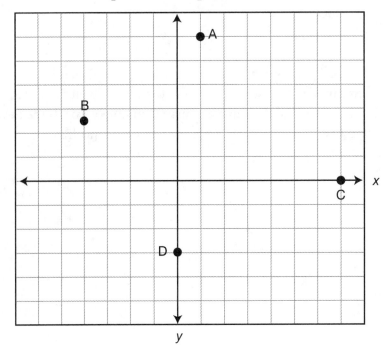

427. •A

428. •B

429. •C

430. •D

Set 88

Plot each point on the same coordinate plane. Remember to label each point appropriately.

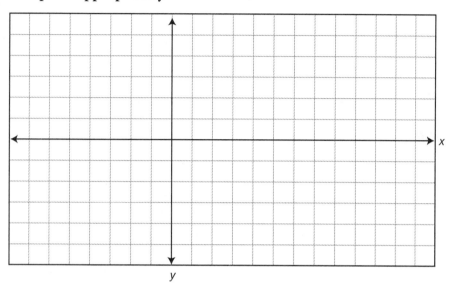

431. From the origin, plot •M (4,5).

432. From the origin, plot •N (12,–1).

433. From the origin, plot •O (–3,–6).

434. From •M, plot •P (0,1).

435. From •N, plot •Q (–4,0).

436. From •O, plot •R (–7,–3).

Set 89

Find the distance between each given pair of points.

437. •A (0,4) and •B (32,0)

438. •C (–2,–1) and •D (4,–1)

439. •E (–3,3) and •F (7,3)

440. •G (17,0) and •H (–3,0)

Answers

Set 86

415. **c.** The origin, whose coordinate pair is (0,0), is in fact a location. It is where the x-axis meets the y-axis. It is not the beginning of either axis because both axes extend infinitely in opposite directions, which means they have no beginning and no end.

416. **c.** Both coordinates are negative: count three spaces left of the origin; then count two spaces down from the x-axis. •A is in quadrant III.

417. **b.** You do not need to actually count 109 spaces left of the origin to know that •M lies left of the y-axis. Nor do you need to count three tenths of a space to know that •M lies above the x-axis. Points left of the y-axis and above the x-axis are in quadrant II.

418. **a.** Again, you do not need to count one-hundredth of a space right of the origin or a hundred spaces up from the x-axis to find in which quadrant •Q lies. To know which quadrant •Q lies in, you only need to know that •Q is right of the y-axis and above the x-axis. Points right of the y-axis and above the x-axis lie in quadrant I.

419. **d.** To find a new coordinate pair, add like coordinates: $3 + (-1) = 2.1 + (-2) = -1$. This new coordinate pair is •R $(2,-1)$; •R lies in quadrant IV.

420. **b.** To find a new coordinate pair, add like coordinates: $(-40) + 20 = -20$. $.02 + .18 = .20$. This new coordinate pair is •B $(-20,.20)$; •B lies in quadrant II.

421. **b.** To find a new coordinate pair, add like coordinates: $15 + (-15) = 0$. $(-15) + 0 = -15$. This new coordinate pair is $(0,-15)$; any point without an x-value lies on the y-axis.

422. **a.** Just as points along the y-axis have no x-value, points along the x-axis have no y-value, and their equation is $y = 0$. Lines on a coordinate plane are still lines: they have no depth. They are not solid lines; and they are infinitely long.

423. **b.** Draw a baseball field—its exact shape is irrelevant; only the alignment of the players matter. They form the axis of the coordinate plane. The ball passes the pitcher and veers left of the second baseman; it is in the second quadrant.

424. **b.** •A, •B, and •C are collinear; they could be connected to make a horizontal line, but they are not a line. Choice **d** is incorrect because all points on a coordinate plane are coplanar.

425. **a.** Three noncollinear points determine a plane. Choices **b** and **d** are incorrect because •G, •H, and •I do not lie on a common line, nor can they be connected to form a straight line. Caution: Do not assume points are noncollinear because they do not share a common x or y coordinate. To be certain, plot the points on a coordinate plane and try to connect them with one straight line.

426. **c.** First, find the difference between like coordinates: $x - x$ and $y - y$: $4 - (-2) = 6$. $-5 - 0 = -5$. Square both differences: $6^2 = 36$. $(-5)^2 = 25$. Remember a negative number multiplied by a negative number is a positive number. Add the squared differences together, and take the square root of their sum: $36 + 25 = 61$. $d = \sqrt{61}$. If you chose choice **a**, then your mistake began after you squared -5; the square of a negative number is positive. If you chose choice **b**, then your mistake began when subtracting the x-coordinates; two negatives make a positive. If you chose **d**, then you didn't square your differences; you doubled your differences.

Set 87

427. •A (1,6). To locate •A from the origin, count one space right of the origin and six spaces up.

428. •B (−4,2.5). To locate •B from the origin, count four spaces left of the origin and two and a half spaces up.

429. **•C (7,0).** To locate •C from the origin, count seven spaces right of the origin and no spaces up or down. This point lies on the x-axis and has no y-value.

430. **•D (0,–3).** To locate •D from the origin, count no spaces left or right, but count 3 spaces down from the origin. This point lies on the y-axis, and x equals zero.

Set 88

For questions 431–436. see the graph below.

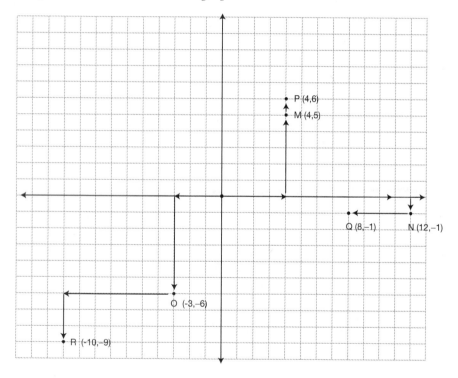

Set 89

437. **Distance = 28.** $d^2 = (0 – 0)^2 + (4 – 32)^2$. $d^2 = 0^2 + (–28)^2$. $d^2 = 784$. $d = 28$. Because these two points form a vertical line, you could just count the number of spaces along the line's length to find the distance between •A and •B.

438. *Distance* = **26.** $d^2 = (-1 - 4)^2 + (-2 - (-1))^2$. $d^2 = (-5)^2 + (-1)^2$. $d^2 = 25 + 1$. $d = \sqrt{26}$.

439. *Distance* = **10.** $d^2 = (-3 - 7)^2 + (3 - 3)^2$. $d^2 = (-10)^2 + 0^2$. $d^2 = 100$. $d = 10$. Again, because these two points form a horizontal line, you could just count the number of spaces along the line's length to find the distance between •E and •F.

440. *Distance* = **20.** $d^2 = (17 - (-3))^2 + (0 - 0)^2$. $d^2 = (20)^2 + 0^2$. $d^2 = 400$. $d = 20$. Because these two points also form a horizontal line, you could just count the spaces along the line's length to find the distance between •G and •H.

18

The Slope of a Line

The SLOPE of a line is the measure of its incline.

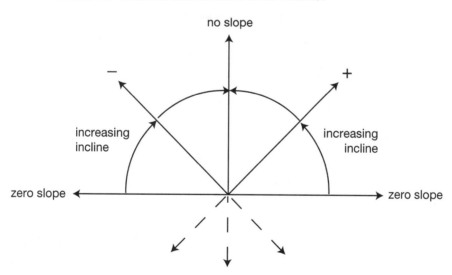

A horizontal line has **zero slope**. As incline increases, slope increases until the line is vertical; the slope of a vertical line is undefined, also called **no slope**. Think of slope as the effort to climb a hill. A horizontal surface is zero effort; a steep hill takes a lot of effort, and a vertical surface cannot be climbed without equipment.

Finding Slope

Slope is represented by a ratio of height to length (the legs of a right triangle), or rise to run. It is written as $\frac{\Delta Y}{\Delta X}$, where ΔY is the change in vertical distance, and ΔX is the change in horizontal distance.

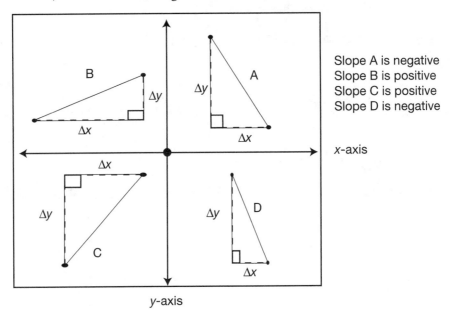

Slope A is negative
Slope B is positive
Slope C is positive
Slope D is negative

Note: Positive and negative slopes indicate direction of an incline. A positive slope rises from left to right. A negative slope descends from left to right, or rises from right to left.

Slope in a Line Equation

Every line on a coordinate plane has a line equation. Most of those line equations have two variables, x and y. You can substitute the coordinate values for every point on that line into the equation and still satisfy the equation. When a line equation is written as $y = mx + b$, the slope of the line is the value of m.

The Slopes of Perpendicular and Parallel Lines

Parallel lines have the **same** slope. Perpendicular lines have **negative reciprocal** slopes. If a slope is $\frac{1}{2}$, a perpendicular slope is -2.

Set 90

Choose the best answer.

441. Pam and Sam are climbing different hills with the same incline. If each hill were graphed, they would have the same
    a. equation.
    b. slope.
    c. length.
    d. coordinates.

442. In American homes, a standard stair rises 7″ for every 9″. The slope of a standard staircase is
    a. $\frac{7}{9}$.
    b. $\frac{2}{7}$.
    c. $\frac{16}{9}$.
    d. $\frac{9}{7}$.

443. Which equation is a line perpendicular to $y = -\frac{1}{2}x + 4$?
    a. $\frac{1}{2}x + 4$
    b. $y = 2x + 8$
    c. $y = -2x + 8$
    d. $y = \frac{1}{2}x + 8$

444. Bethany's ramp to her office lobby rises 3 feet for every 36 feet. The incline is
    a. $\frac{36 \text{ feet}}{1 \text{ foot}}$.
    b. $\frac{12 \text{ feet}}{1 \text{ foot}}$.
    c. $\frac{1 \text{ foot}}{12 \text{ feet}}$.
    d. $\frac{36 \text{ feet}}{3 \text{ feet}}$.

445. Which equation is a line parallel to $y = -\frac{14}{15}x + 7$?

    a. $y = \frac{14}{15}x + 12$

    b. $y = \frac{15}{14}x + 7$

    c. $y = \frac{-14}{15}x + 12$

    d. $y = \frac{15}{14}x + 12$

446. The y-axis has

    a. zero slope.

    b. undefined slope.

    c. positive slope.

    d. negative slope.

Set 91

State the slope for each of the following diagrams.

447.

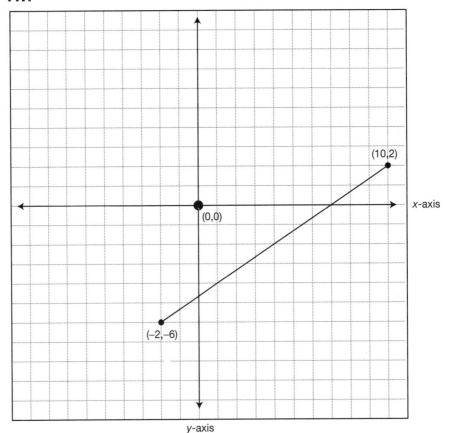

448.

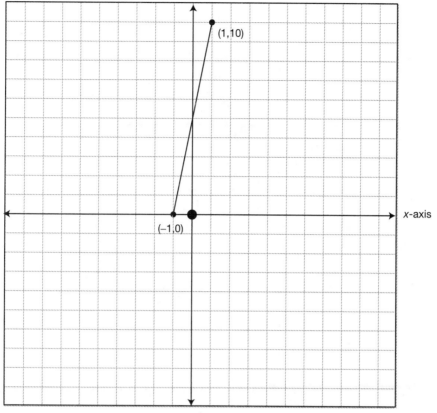

449.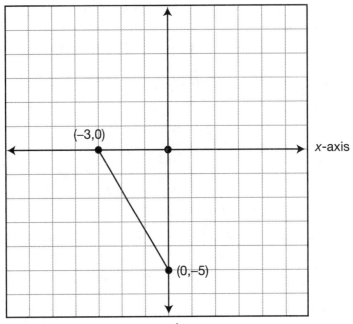

450.

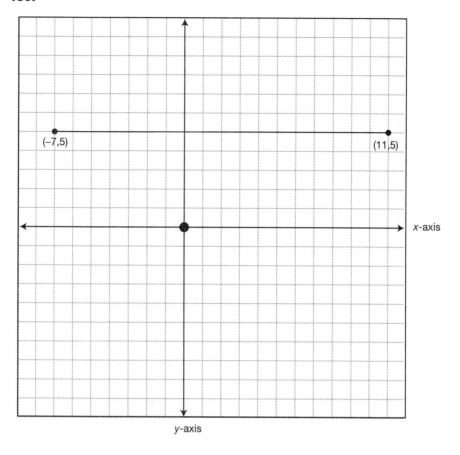

(–7,5)   (11,5)

x-axis

y-axis

Set 92

Draw each line on one coordinate plane.

451. •M (0,6) lies on line *l*, which has a $-\frac{5}{2}$ slope. Draw line *l*.

452. •Q (–3,–4) lies on line *m*, which has a 3 slope. Draw line *m*.

453. •S (9,–2) lies on line *n*, which has a $\frac{1.0}{0.5}$ slope. Draw line *n*.

Set 93

Use distance and slope formulas to prove the validity of questions 454 through 456.

454. Show that the figure with vertices A (2,–5), B (6,–1), and C (6,–5) is a right triangle.

455. Show that the figure with vertices A (–8,3), B (–6,5), C (4,5), and D (2, 3) is a parallelogram.

456. Show that the figure with vertices A (–5,–5), B (–5,–1), C (–1,–1), and D (–1,–7) is a trapezoid.

Answers

Set 90

441. **b.** If two lines have the same incline, they rise the same amount over the same distance; the relationship of rise over distance is slope.

442. **a.** If every step rises 7″ for every 9″, then the relationship of rise over distance is $\frac{7}{9}$.

443. **b.** In the slope-intercept formula, the constant preceding the variable x is the line's slope. If perpendicular lines have slopes that are negative reciprocals, a line perpendicular to $y = -\frac{1}{2}x + 4$ must have a $\frac{2}{1}$ slope.

444. **c.** If the ramp rises 3 feet for every 36 feet, then the relationship of rise over distance is $\frac{3 \text{ foot}}{36 \text{ feet}}$. The simplified ratio is $\frac{1 \text{ foot}}{12 \text{ feet}}$.

445. **c.** Parallel lines have the same rise over distance ratio, or slope. That means in slope-intercept equations, the constant before the x-variable will be the same. In this case, $-\frac{14}{15}$ must precede x in both equations. Choices **b** and **d** are perpendicular line equations because their slopes are negative reciprocals of the given slope. Choice **a** is an entirely different line.

446. **b.** The y-axis is a vertical line; its slope is $\frac{1}{0}$ or undefined (sometimes referred to as "no slope"). The x-axis is an example of a horizontal line; horizontal lines have zero slope. Positive slopes are non-vertical lines that rise from left to right; negative slopes are non-vertical lines that descend from left to right.

Set 91

447. $\frac{2}{3}$. Subtract like coordinates: $-2 - 10 = -12$. $-6 - 2 = -8$. Place the vertical change in distance over the horizontal change in distance: $\frac{-8}{-12}$. Then reduce the top and bottom of the fraction by 4. The final slope is $\frac{2}{3}$.

448. **5.** Subtract like coordinates: $-1 - 1 = -2$. $0 - 10 = -10$. Place the vertical change in distance over the horizontal change in distance: $-\frac{10}{-2}$. Then reduce the top and bottom of the fraction by 2. The final slope is 5.

449. $-\frac{5}{3}$. Subtract like coordinates: $-3 - 0 = -3$. $0 - (-5) = 5$. Place the vertical change in distance over the horizontal change in distance: $\frac{5}{-3}$. The slope is $-\frac{5}{3}$.

450. **0 (zero slope).** Horizontal lines have zero slope ($\frac{0}{-18} = 0$).

Set 92

For questions 451–453, see the graph below.

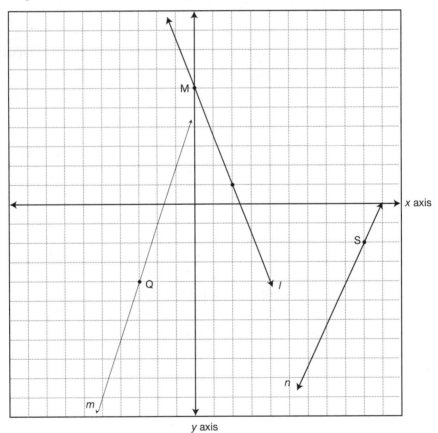

Set 93

454. You could draw the figure, or you could find the slope between each line. The slope of $\overline{AB}$ is $\frac{(-5-(-1))}{(2-6)}$, or $\frac{4}{-4}$. The slope of $\overline{BC}$ is $\frac{(-1-(-5))}{(6-6)}$, or $\frac{-6}{0}$. The slope of $\overline{CA}$ is $\frac{(-5-(-5))}{(6-2)}$, or $\frac{0}{4}$. $\overline{BC}$ is vertical because its slope is undefined; $\overline{CA}$ is horizontal because its slope equals zero. Horizontal and vertical lines meet perpendicularly; therefore $\triangle ABC$ is a right triangle.

455. Again, you could draw figure ABCD in a coordinate plane and visually confirm that it is a parallelogram, or you could find the slope and distance between each point. The slope of $\overline{AB}$ is $\frac{(3-5)}{(-8-(-6))}$, or $\frac{2}{2}$. The distance between •A and •B is $\sqrt{(-2)^2+(-2)^2}$, or $2\sqrt{2}$. The slope of $\overline{BC}$ is $\frac{(5-5)}{(-6-4)}$, or $\frac{0}{-10}$. The distance between •B and •C is the difference of the x coordinates, or 10. The slope of $\overline{CD}$ is $\frac{(5-3)}{(4-2)}$, or $\frac{2}{2}$. The distance between •C and •D is $\sqrt{2^2+2^2}$, or $2\sqrt{2}$. The slope of line $\overline{DA}$ is $\frac{(3-3)}{(-8-2)}$, or $\frac{0}{10}$. The distance between •D and •A is the difference of the x-coordinates, or 10. From the calculations above you know that opposite $\overline{AB}$ and $\overline{CD}$ have the same slope and length, which means they are parallel and congruent. Also opposite lines $\overline{BC}$ and $\overline{DA}$ have the same zero slope and lengths; again, they are parallel and congruent; therefore figure ABCD is a parallelogram because opposite sides $\overline{AB}/\overline{CD}$ and $\overline{BC}/\overline{DA}$ are parallel and congruent.

456. You must prove that only one pair of opposite sides in figure ABCD is parallel and noncongruent. Slope AB is $\frac{-4}{0}$; its length is the difference of y coordinates, or 4. Slope $\overline{BC}$ is $\frac{0}{-4}$; its length is the difference of x coordinates, or 4. Slope of $\overline{CD}$ is $\frac{6}{0}$; its length is the difference of y coordinates, or 6. Finally, slope of $\overline{DA}$ is $(\frac{-1}{2})$; its length is $\sqrt{4^2+(-2^2)}$, or $2\sqrt{5}$. Opposite sides $\overline{AB}$ and $\overline{CD}$ have the same slope but measure different lengths; therefore they are parallel and noncongruent. Figure ABCD is a trapezoid.

19

The Equation of a Line

The standard linear line equation is $ax + by = c$. It has no exponents greater than one and at least one variable (x or y).

Points on a Line

Every point on a line will satisfy the line's equation. To find whether a point satisfies the equation, plug it in. To find points along a line, use a single variable. Plug it in and solve for the unknown coordinate. Using a chart to monitor your progress will help you.

x	$-2x + 1y = -1$	y
1	$-2(1) + 1y = -1$ $-2 \quad + \ y = -1$ $+2 \qquad\qquad +2$ $y = \ \ 1$	1
0	$-2(0) + 1y = -1$ $0 \ + \ y = -1$ $y = -1$	-1
-1	$-2(-1) + 1y = -1$ $+2 \quad + \ y = -1$ $-2 \qquad\qquad -2$ $y = -3$	-3

The Slope-Intercept Equation

A special arrangement of the linear equation looks like $y = mx + b$. m represents the line's slope. b represents the y coordinate where the line crosses the y-axis.

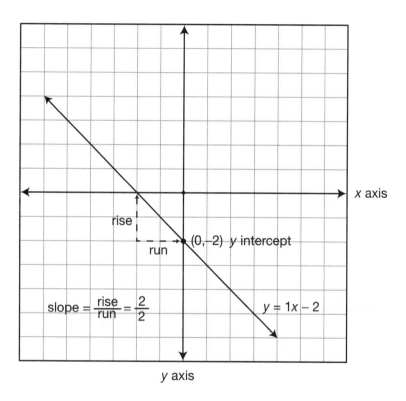

Set 94

Choose the best answer.

457. In the linear equation $y = -4x + 5$, the y-intercept is
    a. (5,0).
    b. (−4,0).
    c. (0,−4).
    d. (0,5).

458. The slope of linear equation $y = \frac{2}{3}x - 1$ is
a. 2.
b. $\frac{2}{3}$.
c. $\frac{3}{2}$.
d. 3.

459. What is the value of b if $(-2,3)$ satisfies the equation $y = \frac{1}{2}x + b$.
a. -2
b. -1
c. 3
d. 4

460. What is the value of y if $(1,y)$ satisfies the equation $y = -\frac{12}{5}x + \frac{2}{5}$.
a. 1
b. -2
c. -3
d. -1

461. Convert the linear equation $4x - 2y = 4$ into a slope-intercept equation.
2. $y = 2x - 2$
b. $y = -2x + 2$
c. $x = \frac{1}{2}y - 2$
d. $x = -\frac{1}{2}y + 2$

462. •A $(-4,0)$, •B $(0,3)$, and •C $(8,9)$ satisfy which equation?
a. $y = \frac{4}{3}x + 3$
b. $y = \frac{3}{4}x + 0$
c. $y = \frac{3}{4}x + 3$
d. $y = \frac{6}{8}x + 9$

463. Find the missing y value if •A, •B, and •C are collinear: •A $(-3,-1)$, •B $(0,y)$, and •C $(3,-9)$.
a. 1
b. -1
c. -3
d. -5

464. Which line perpendicularly meets line $1x + 2y = 4$ on the y-axis?
    a. $y = -\frac{1}{2}x + 2$
    b. $y = 2x + 2$
    c. $y = -2x - 2$
    d. $y = \frac{1}{2}x - 2$

465. A $(0, -2)$ satisfies which equation that parallels $\frac{1}{2}x + \frac{1}{4}y = \frac{1}{8}$?
    a. $y = 2x + \frac{1}{2}$
    b. $y = \frac{1}{2}x + \frac{1}{2}$
    c. $y = -2x - 2$
    d. $y = -2x + \frac{1}{2}$

Set 95

A **point of interception** is a point in space shared by two or more lines. **At a point of interception, line equations are equal.**

For each set of equations below, find the point of interception.

466. $y = \frac{1}{2}x + 4$
     $y = -4x + 1$

467. $y = -\frac{6}{5}x - \frac{1}{2}$
     $y = 1x + 1$

468. $\frac{1}{2}y = 2x + 6$
     $y = -\frac{1}{3}x - \frac{1}{3}$

469. $y = 10x - 2$
     $y + 3 = \frac{4}{5}x$

470. $1x + 2y = 4$
     $\frac{5}{2}x - y = \frac{1}{2}$

Set 96

Use the line equations below to answer questions 471 through 474.

$x = 0$
$y = 0$
$y = x - 3.$

471. What are the vertices of $\triangle ABC$?

472. What is the special name for $\triangle ABC$?

473. What is the perimeter of $\triangle ABC$?

474. What is the area of $\triangle ABC$?

Set 97

Use the line equations below to answer questions 475 through 479.

$y = -\frac{1}{3}x - 3$
$y = \frac{1}{3}x - 1$
$y = -\frac{1}{3}x - 1$
$y = \frac{1}{3}x - 3$

475. What are the vertices of quadrilateral ABCD?

476. Show that quadrilateral ABCD is a parallelogram.

477. Show that diagonals $\overline{AC}$ and $\overline{BD}$ perpendicular.

478. What special parallelogram is quadrilateral ABCD?

479. What is the area of quadrilateral ABCD?

Answers

Set 94

457. **d.** When a line intercepts the y-axis, its x value is always zero. Immediately, choices **a** and **b** are eliminated. In the slope-y intercept equation, the number without a variable beside it is the y value of the y intercept coordinate pair. Choice **c** is eliminated because −4 is actually the line's slope value.

458. **b.** In the slope-y intercept equation, the number preceding the x variable is the line's slope. In this case that number is the entire fraction $\frac{2}{3}$.

459. **d.** Plug the value of x and y into the equation and solve: $3 = \frac{1}{2}(-2) + b$. $3 = (-1) + b$. $4 = b$.

460. **b.** Plug the value of x into the equation and solve: $y = -\frac{12}{5}(1) + \frac{2}{5} \cdot y = -\frac{12}{5} + \frac{2}{5} \cdot y = -\frac{10}{5} \cdot y = -2$.

461. **a.** To convert a standard linear equation into a slope-intercept equation, single out the y variable. Subtract $4x$ from both sides: $-2y = -4x + 4$. Divide both sides by -2: $y = 2x - 2$. Choices **c** and **d** are incorrect because they single out the x variable. Choice **b** is incorrect because after both sides of the equation are divided by -2, the signs were not reversed on the right hand side.

462. **c.** Find the slope between any two of the given points: $\frac{(0-3)}{(-4-0)} = \frac{-3}{-4}$, or $\frac{3}{4}$. •B is the y intercept. Plug the slope and y value of •B into the formula $y = mx + b$. $y = \frac{3}{4}x + 3$.

463. **d.** The unknown y value is also the intercept value of a line that connects all three points. First, find the slope between •A and •C: $-3 - 3 = -6$. $-1 - (-9) = 8$. $-\frac{6}{8}$, or $-\frac{3}{4}$ represents the slope. From •A, count right three spaces and down four spaces. You are at point $(0,-5)$. From this point, count right three spaces and down four spaces. You are at point $(3,-9)$. Point $(0,-5)$ is on the line connecting •A and •C; -5 is your unknown value.

464. **b.** First, convert the standard linear equation into a slope-y intercept equation. Isolate the y variable: $2y = -1x + 4$. Divide both sides by 2: $y = -\frac{1}{2}x + 2$. A line that perpendicularly intercepts this line on the y-axis has a negative reciprocal slope but has the same y intercept value: $y = 2x + 2$.

465. **c.** First, convert the standard linear equation into a slope-intercept equation. Isolate the y variable: $\frac{1}{4}y = -\frac{1}{2}x + \frac{1}{8}$. Multiply both sides by 4: $y = -2x + \frac{1}{2}$. A parallel line will have the same slope as the given equation; however the y intercept will be different: $y = -2x - 2$.

466. $(-\frac{2}{3}, \frac{11}{3})$. Line up equations and solve for x: $\frac{1}{2}x + 4 = -4x + 1$. $\frac{1}{2}x + 4x = -3$. $\frac{9}{2}x = -3$. $x = -\frac{2}{3}$. Insert the value of x into one equation and solve for y: $y = \frac{1}{2}(-\frac{2}{3}) + 4$. $y = -\frac{1}{3} + 4$. $y = \frac{11}{3}$. To check your answer, plug the x and y value into the second equation. $\frac{11}{3} = -4(-\frac{2}{3}) + 1$. $\frac{11}{3} = \frac{8}{3} + \frac{3}{3}$. $\frac{11}{3} = \frac{11}{3}$. If opposite sides of the equal sign are the same, then your solution is correct.

467. $(-\frac{15}{22}, \frac{7}{22})$. Line up equations and solve for x: $-\frac{6}{5}x - \frac{1}{2} = 1x + 1$. $\frac{6}{5}x - 1x = \frac{1}{2} + 1$. $-\frac{11}{5}x = \frac{3}{2}$. $x = -\frac{15}{22}$. Insert the value of x into one equation and solve: $y = -\frac{15}{22} + 1$. $y = \frac{7}{22}$.

468. $(-\frac{37}{13}, \frac{8}{13})$. First, rearrange the first equation so that only the variable y is on one side of the equal sign. $y = \frac{2}{1}(2x + 6)$. $y = 4x + 12$. Line up equations and solve for x: $4x + 12 = -\frac{1}{3}x - \frac{1}{3}$. $4x + \frac{1}{3}x = -12 - \frac{1}{3}$. $\frac{13}{3}x = -\frac{37}{3}$. $x = -\frac{37}{13}$. Insert the value of x into one equation and solve for y: $\frac{1}{2}y = 2(-\frac{37}{13}) + 6$. $\frac{1}{2}y = -\frac{74}{13} + \frac{78}{13}$. $\frac{1}{2}y = \frac{4}{13}$. $y = \frac{8}{13}$.

469. $(-\frac{5}{46}, -\frac{71}{23})$. First, rearrange the second equation so that only the variable y is on one side of the equal sign: $y = \frac{4}{5}x - 3$. Line up equations and solve for x: $\frac{4}{5}x - 3 = 10x - 2$. $\frac{4}{5}x - 10x = 3 - 2$. $-\frac{46}{5}x = 1$. $x = -\frac{5}{46}$. Insert the value of x into one equation and solve for y: $y = 10(-\frac{5}{46}) - 2$. $y = -\frac{50}{46} - \frac{92}{46}$. $y = -\frac{142}{46}$. $y = -\frac{71}{23}$.

470. $(\frac{5}{6}, \frac{19}{12})$. First, rearrange both equations to read, "y equals": $2y = 4 -$
x. $y = 2 - \frac{1}{2}x$; $-y = \frac{1}{2} - \frac{5}{2}x$. $y = -\frac{1}{2} + \frac{5}{2}x$. Line up equations and
solve for x: $2 - \frac{1}{2}x = -\frac{1}{2} + \frac{5}{2}x$. $2 + \frac{1}{2} = \frac{1}{2}x + \frac{5}{2}x$. $\frac{5}{2} = \frac{6}{2}x$. $\frac{5}{6} = x$. Insert
the value of x into one equation and solve: $\frac{5}{6} + 2y = 4$. $2y = \frac{24}{6} - \frac{5}{6}$.
$2y = \frac{19}{6} = \frac{19}{12}$.

Set 95

471. •A (0,0), •B (3,0), and •C (0,3). Usually, in pairs, you would solve
for each point of interception; however, $x = 0$ (the y-axis) and $y = 0$
(the x-axis) meet at the origin; therefore the origin is the first point
of interception. One at a time, plug $x = 0$ and $y = 0$ into the
equation $y = x - 3$ to find the two other points of interception: $y = 0$
$- 3$. $y = -3$; and $0 = x - 3$. $3 = x$. The vertices of $\triangle ABC$ are A (0, 0),
B (3,0), and C (0,3).

472. **$\triangle ABC$ is an isosceles right triangle.** $\overline{AB}$ has zero slope; $\overline{CA}$ has
no slope, or undefined slope. They are perpendicular, and they
both measure 3 lengths. $\triangle ABC$ is an isosceles right triangle.

473. *Perimeter* **= 6 units + $3\sqrt{2}$ units.** $\overline{AB}$ and $\overline{CA}$ are three units
long. Using the Pythagorean theorem or the distance formula, find
the length of $\overline{BC}$. $d = \sqrt{3^2 + 3^2}$. $d = \sqrt{18}$. $d = 3\sqrt{2}$. The
perimeter of $\triangle ABC$ is the sum of the lengths of its sides: $3 + 3 +$
$3\sqrt{2} = 6 + 3\sqrt{2}$.

474. *Area* **= 4.5 square units.** The area of $\triangle ABC$ is $\frac{1}{2}$ its height times
its length, or $\frac{1}{2}(3 \times 3)$. $a = 4.5$ square units.

Set 96

475. In pairs, find each point of interception:

•A $(-3,-2)$. $-\frac{1}{3}x - 3 = \frac{1}{3}x - 1$. $-\frac{1}{3}x - \frac{1}{3}x = 3 - 1$. $-\frac{2}{3}x = 2$. $x = -3$;
$y = -\frac{1}{3}(-3) - 3$. $y = 1 - 3$. $y = -2$.

•B $(0,-1)$. $\frac{1}{3}x - 1 = -\frac{1}{3}x - 1$. $\frac{1}{3}x + \frac{1}{3}x = 1 - 1$. $\frac{2}{3}x = 0$. $x = 0$;
$y = \frac{1}{3}(0) - 1$. $y = -1$.

•C $(3,-2)$. $-\frac{1}{3}x - 1 = \frac{1}{3}x - 3$. $-\frac{1}{3}x - \frac{1}{3}x = 1 - 3$. $-\frac{2}{3}x = -2$. $x = 3$;
$y = -\frac{1}{3}(3) - 1$. $y = -1 - 1$. $y = -2$.

•D $(0,-3)$. $\frac{1}{3}x - 3 = -\frac{1}{3}x - 3$. $\frac{1}{3}x + \frac{1}{3}x = 3 - 3$. $\frac{2}{3}x = 0$. $x = 0$;
$y = \frac{1}{3}(0) - 3$. $y = -3$.

476. In slope-intercept form, the slope is the constant preceding x. You can very quickly determine that $\overline{AB}$ and $\overline{CD}$, and $\overline{BC}$, and $\overline{DA}$ have the same slopes. The length of each line segment is:

$m\text{AB} = \sqrt{10}$. $d = \sqrt{(-3 - 0)^2 + (-2 - -1)^2}$. $d = \sqrt{9 + 1}$. $d = \sqrt{10}$.

$m\text{BC} = \sqrt{10}$. $d = \sqrt{(0 - 3)^2 + (-1 - -2)^2}$. $d = \sqrt{9 + 1}$. $d = \sqrt{10}$.

$m\text{CD} = \sqrt{10}$. $d = \sqrt{(3 - 0)^2 + (-2 - -3)^2}$. $d = \sqrt{9 + 1}$. $d = \sqrt{10}$.

$m\text{CA} = \sqrt{10}$. $d = \sqrt{(0 - -3)^2 + (-3 - -2)^2}$. $d = \sqrt{9 + 1}$. $d = \sqrt{10}$.

477. The slope of a line is the change in y over the change in x. The slope of $\overline{AC}$ is $\frac{-2 - (-2)}{-3 - 3}$, or $\frac{0}{-6}$. The slope of $\overline{BD}$ is $\frac{-1 - (-3)}{0 - 0}$, or $\frac{2}{0}$. Lines with zero slopes and no slopes are perpendicular; therefore diagonals $\overline{AC}$ and $\overline{BD}$ are perpendicular.

478. Rhombus. Quadrilateral ABCD is a rhombus because opposite sides are parallel, all four sides are congruent, and diagonals are perpendicular.

479. *Area* = **12 square units.** The area of a rhombus is its base times its height or the product of its diagonals. In this case, the product of its diagonals is the easiest to find because the diagonals are vertical and horizontal lines. $\overline{AC}$ is 6 units long while $\overline{BD}$ is 2 units long: 6 units $\times$ 2 units = 12 square units.

20

Trigonometry Basics

Geometry provides the foundation for trigonometry. Look at the triangles on the next page. They are right similar triangles: their corresponding angles are congruent and their corresponding sides are in proportion to each other.

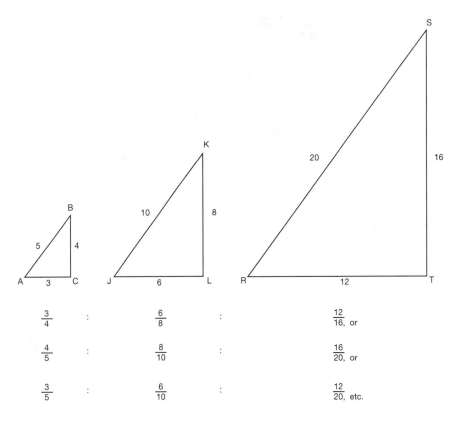

$$\frac{3}{4} \qquad : \qquad \frac{6}{8} \qquad : \qquad \frac{12}{16}, \text{ or}$$

$$\frac{4}{5} \qquad : \qquad \frac{8}{10} \qquad : \qquad \frac{16}{20}, \text{ or}$$

$$\frac{3}{5} \qquad : \qquad \frac{6}{10} \qquad : \qquad \frac{12}{20}, \text{ etc.}$$

Create a ratio using any two sides of just the first triangle. Compare that ratio to another ratio using the corresponding sides of the triangle next of it. They are equal. Compare these two ratios to the next similar triangle. All three are equal, and they always will be.

Unlike the Pythagorean theorem, trigonometric ratios do not call the legs of a right triangle *a* or *b*. Instead, they are called **adjacent** or **opposite** to an angle in the right triangle.

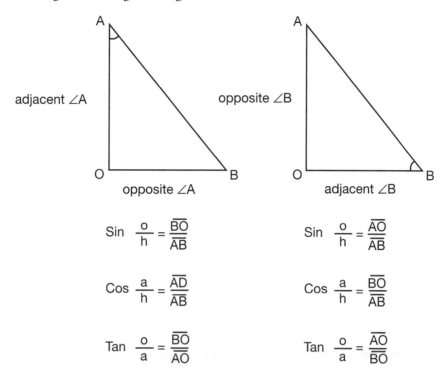

Sin $\dfrac{o}{h} = \dfrac{\overline{BO}}{\overline{AB}}$ Sin $\dfrac{o}{h} = \dfrac{\overline{AO}}{\overline{AB}}$

Cos $\dfrac{a}{h} = \dfrac{\overline{AD}}{\overline{AB}}$ Cos $\dfrac{a}{h} = \dfrac{\overline{BO}}{\overline{AB}}$

Tan $\dfrac{o}{a} = \dfrac{\overline{BO}}{\overline{AO}}$ Tan $\dfrac{o}{a} = \dfrac{\overline{AO}}{\overline{BO}}$

Each combination of sides has a special name:

$$\text{Sine } \angle = \frac{\text{opposite leg}}{\text{hypotenuse}}, \text{ or Sin } \angle = \frac{o}{h}$$

$$\text{Cosine } \angle = \frac{\text{adjacent leg}}{\text{hypotenuse}}, \text{ or Cos } \angle = \frac{a}{h}$$

$$\text{Tangent } \angle = \frac{\text{opposite leg}}{\text{adjacent leg}}, \text{ or Tan } \angle = \frac{o}{a}$$

(If you can remember this phrase, then you will remember
the order of each ratio:
"<u>O</u> Heck, <u>A</u>nother <u>H</u>our <u>O</u>f <u>A</u>lgebra")

Using a Trigonometric Table

Trigonometric ratios for all acute angles are commonly listed in tables. Scientific calculators also have functions for the trigonometric ratios. Consult your calculator handbook to make sure you have your calculator in the *degree*, and not the *radian* setting. Part of a trigonometric table is given below.

Angle	Sin	Cos	Tan
16°	0.276	0.961	0.287
17°	0.292	0.956	0.306
18°	0.309	0.951	0.325
19°	0.326	0.946	0.344
20°	0.342	0.940	0.364
21°	0.358	0.934	0.384
22°	0.375	0.927	0.404
23°	0.391	0.921	0.424
24°	0.407	0.914	0.445
25°	0.423	0.906	0.466
26°	0.438	0.899	0.488
27°	0.454	0.891	0.510
28°	0.470	0.883	0.532
29°	0.485	0.875	0.554
30°	0.500	0.866	0.577
31°	0.515	0.857	0.601
32°	0.530	0.848	0.625
33°	0.545	0.839	0.649
34°	0.559	0.829	0.675
35°	0.574	0.819	0.700
36°	0.588	0.809	0.727
37°	0.602	0.799	0.754
38°	0.616	0.788	0.781
39°	0.629	0.777	0.810
40°	0.643	0.766	0.839
41°	0.656	0.755	0.869
42°	0.669	0.743	0.900
43°	0.682	0.731	0.933
44°	0.695	0.719	0.966
45°	0.707	0.707	1.000

Example: Find each value.
a. cos 44°
b. tan 42°

Solution:
a. cos 44° = 0.719
b. tan 42° = 0.900

Example: Find $m\angle A$.
a. sin A = 0.656
b. cos A = 0.731

Solution:
a. $m\angle A$ = 41°
b. $m\angle A$ = 43°

Angles and Their Trigonometric Ratio

A trigonometric ratio can determine either of a triangle's acute angles. First, choose the trigonometric function that addresses the angle you are looking for and uses the sides given.

In $\triangle ABC$, $\overline{AB}$ is 5 inches and $\overline{BC}$ is 10 inches. Vertex A is a right angle. What is the rotation of $\angle B$?

$$\text{Cos B} = \frac{\text{adjacent}}{\text{hypotenuse}}$$

$$\text{Cos B} = \frac{5}{10}$$

Divide the ratio into its decimal equivalent; then find the decimal equivalent on the trigonometric chart under the trigonometric function you used (sin, cos, or tan).

$$\text{Cos B} = 0.500$$

$$m\angle B = 60$$

How to Find a Side Using a Trigonometric Ratio and Angle

If one side and an angle are given in a right triangle and a second side is unknown, determine the relationship of both sides to the given angle. Select the appropriate trigonometric function and find its decimal value on the chart. Then solve.

In $\triangle ABC$, $\overline{BC}$ is 20 inches and $\angle B$ is 30°. $\angle A$ is a right angle. Find the length of side CA.

$$\text{Sin } 30 = \frac{\text{opposite}}{\text{hypotenuse}}$$

$$\text{Sin } 30 = \frac{CA}{20}$$

$$0.500 = \frac{CA}{20}$$

$$10 = CA$$

Set 98

Choose the best answer. Trigonometric ratios are rounded to the nearest thousandth.

480. Sin A = $\frac{12}{16}$ is

   a.

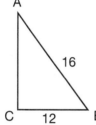

   b.

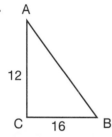

   c.

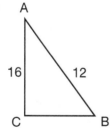

   d.

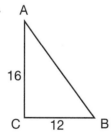

481.   Tan A = $\frac{13}{12}$ is

a.

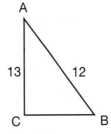

b.

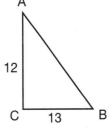

c.

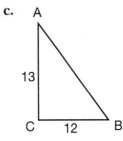

d.

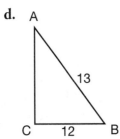

482. Cos B = $\frac{31}{33}$ is

a.

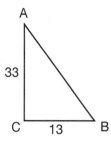

b.

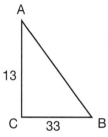

c.

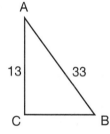

d.

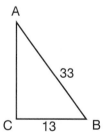

483. Which trigonometric function can equal or be greater than 1,000?
   a. Sine
   b. Cosine
   c. Tangent
   d. none of the above

484. A plane ascends at a 40° angle. When it reaches an altitude of one
hundred feet, how much ground distance has it covered? To solve,
use the trigonometric chart. Round the answer to the nearest
tenth.
   a. 64.3 feet
   b. 76.6 feet
   c. 80.1 feet
   d. 119.2 feet

485. Betty skydives at 4,500 feet. She touches ground 2,000 feet from
the point of departure. What was the angle of her descent?
   a. 24°
   b. 26°
   c. 64°
   d. 66°

486. Which set of angles has the same trigonometric ratio?
   a. Sin 45 and tan 45
   b. Sin 30 and cos 60
   c. Cos 30 and tan 45
   d. Tan 60 and sin 45

487. What is the sum of trigonometric ratios Sin 54 and Cos 36?
   a. 0.809
   b. 1.618
   c. 1.000
   d. 1.536

488. What is the sum of trigonometric ratios Sin 33 and Sin 57?
   a. 0.545
   b. 1.000
   c. 1.090
   d. 1.384

489. What is the sum of trigonometric ratios Cos 16 and Cos 74?
   a. 0.276
   b. 0.961
   c. 1.237
   d. 1.922

490. In △ABC, vertex C is a right angle. Which trigonometric ratio has the same trigonometric value as Sin A?
   a. Sin B
   b. Cosine A
   c. Cosine B
   d. Tan A

491. In △ABC, Tan ∠A = $\frac{3}{4}$. The hypotenuse of △ABC is
   a. 3.
   b. 4.
   c. 5.
   d. 9.

492. In △ABC, Sin ∠B = $\frac{14}{17}$. The hypotenuse of △ABC is
   a. 14.
   b. 17.
   c. $\sqrt{485}$.
   d. 0.824.

493. In △ABC, Cos ∠C is $\frac{22}{36}$. The hypotenuse is
   a. 22.
   b. 36.
   c. 0.611.
   d. $2\sqrt{445}$.

Set 99

Circle whether each answer is True or False.

494. Sine, cosine, and tangent measure acute and obtuse angles.
   True or False

495. The sum of the sine of an angle and the cosine of its complement is always greater than 1.000.   **True or False**

496. The trigonometric ratio of sin 45, cos 45, and tan 45 are equal.
   True or False

Set 100

Use the figure below to answer questions 497 through 500. Trigonometric ratios are rounded to the nearest thousandth.

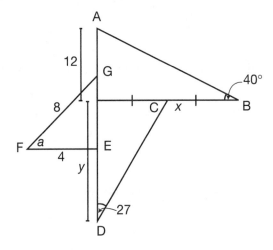

497. What is the length of x?

498. What is the length of y?

499. What is the rotation of $\angle A$?

500. What is the sum of Sin A and Sin G?

Set 101

Use the figure below to answer question 501. Trigonometric ratios are rounded to the nearest thousandth.

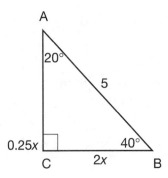

501. What is the value of x?

Answers

Set 98

480. **a.** The trigonometric ratio sine is the length of the side opposite an angle over the length of the hypotenuse (the side opposite the right angle).

481. **b.** The trigonometric ratio tangent is the length of the side opposite an angle over the length of the side adjacent to the angle.

482. **d.** The trigonometric ratio cosine is the length of the side adjacent to an angle over the hypotenuse (the side opposite the right angle).

483. **c.** The trigonometric ratios sine and cosine never equal or exceed 1.000 because the hypotenuse, the longest side of a right triangle, is always their denominator. The trigonometric ratio Tangent can equal and exceed the value 1.000 because the hypotenuse is never its denominator.

484. **d.** The question seeks the length of a leg adjacent to $\angle 40$. Your only option is the trigonometric ratio tan. The trigonometric value of tan 40 is 0.839: $0.839 = \frac{100 \text{ feet}}{a}$. $a = 119.2$ feet.

485. **a.** The problem provides the lengths of two legs and an unknown angle. You could solve for a hypotenuse using the Pythagorean theorem, and then use sine or cosine. But the least amount of work uses what the question provides. Only the trigonometric ratio tan uses the lengths of two legs. Divide 2,000 by 4,500 and match the answer on the chart.

486. **b.** Observe the ratios formed by a 30-60-90 triangle: Sin A is opposite over hypotenuse. Cos B is adjacent over hypotenuse. What is opposite $\angle A$ is adjacent to $\angle B$. The ratio is exactly the same. The sin and cosine of opposite or complementary angles are equal (example: sin 21 and cos 69, sin 52 and cos 38).

487. **b.** The value of sin 54 is the same as cos 36 because they are the sine/cosine of complementary angles. 2 times 0.809 is 1.618.

488. **d.** Look up the trigonometric values of sin 33 and sin 57. Add their values together. However, if your trigonometric chart does not cover 57°, you could trace the trigonometric values of sin 33 and cos 33, add them together and arrive at the same answer because cos 33 is equivalent to sin 57.

489. **c.** Look up the values of cos 16° and the cos of 74°, and add them together. If your chart does not cover 74°, look up the values of cos 16° and the sin of 16°.

490. **c.** Choices **b** and **c** are the same angle as the given. Choice **a** uses the side adjacent to ∠A; that creates an entirely different ratio from sin A. Only choice **c** uses the side opposite ∠A (except it is called the side adjacent ∠B).

491. **c.** The trigonometric ratio tan does not include the hypotenuse. It must be solved by using the Pythagorean theorem: $3^2 + 4^2 = c^2$. $25 = c^2$. $5 = c$.

492. **b.** Sine is the length of the side opposite an angle over the length of the hypotenuse; consequently, the answer is the denominator of the given fraction. Choice **d** is the same ratio expressed as decimals.

493. **b.** Cosine is the length of the side adjacent to an angle over the length of the hypotenuse. Again, the hypotenuse and longest side is always the denominator.

Set 99

494. **False.** Sine, cosine, and tangent only measure the acute angles formed in a right triangle.

495. **False.** Individually, the trigonometric values of sine and cosine never exceed 1.0; the sum of either the sines or the cosines of complementary angles always exceeds 1.0; but the sine of an angle and the cosine of its complement do not always exceed 1.0. Try it:

Sin 17 + Sin 73 = 1.248. Cos 44 + Cos 46 = 1.414.

Sin 17 + Cos 73 = 0.584. Cos 44 + Sin 46 = 1.438.

496. **False**. Only sine and cosine have the same trigonometric ratio value at 45°. At 45°, the trigonometric ratio tan equals 1.

Set 100

497. $x \approx 14.303$. Using the angle given (you can use $\angle A$; as $\angle B$'s complement, it measures 50°), $\overline{AE}$ is opposite $\angle B$, and $\overline{BE}$ is adjacent $\angle B$. Tan 40 = opposite/adjacent. Tan 40 = $\frac{12}{a}$. 0.839 = $\frac{12}{a}$. a (to the nearest thousandth) ≈ 14.303.

498. $y \approx 14.024$. Half of $\overline{BE}$ is $\overline{CE}$, or half of 14.303 is 7.152. Judging the relationships of each side to $\angle D$ (again, you could use $\angle C$), $\overline{CE}$ is opposite it and $\overline{DE}$ is adjacent it. Tan 27 = opposite/adjacent. Tan 27 = $\frac{7.152}{a}$. 0.510 = $\frac{7.152}{a}$. a (to the nearest thousandth) ≈ 14.024.

499. $m\angle a = 60$. $\overline{FG}$ is a hypotenuse while $\overline{EF}$ is a side adjacent to $\angle a$. Cos a = adjacent/hypotenuse. Cos $a = \frac{4}{8}$. Cos $a = 0.500$. $m\angle a = 60$.

500. *sum* $\angle$ **1.266**. The sum of sin 50 and sin 30 is 0.766 plus 0.500, or 1.266.

Set 101

501. You can use either angle and any three of the trigonometric ratios. To demonstrate an answer, we chose sin 20 = opposite/hypotenuse. Sin 20 = $\frac{2x}{5}$. 0.342 = 0.400x. $x \approx 0.855$.